Please return/renew this item by the last date shown.
Items may also be renewed by the internet*

https://library.eastriding.gov.uk

* Please note a PIN will be required to access this service
- this can be obtained from your library

The National Trust
TOUR OF BRITAIN

THE
MIDLANDS

We start our tour in the heart of England. In the Midlands you'll find monuments of every age, along with areas that escaped the human desire to build and create.

Ask people what comes to mind when they think of the Midlands, and you might get answers ranging from Ironbridge to Ambridge, scenes of heavy industry and everyday stories of country folk.

It's true that the Industrial Revolution transformed the landscape of the Midlands, as it did across the country. Enormous wealth helped create mansions intended to impress and house beautiful collections, but every estate relied on its workers. Grand country houses are full of beauty and history, but there are treasures of a different sort and fascinating glimpses into the past in the homes of those who lived by more modest means.

Nature, too, is on display with wild, untended heathland as well as gardens and parkland, where horticultural ambitions knew no bounds.

All this variety is to be found in the Midlands with more than a few surprises along the way.

Previous pages: View of Quarry Bank, the eighteenth-century cotton mill powered by the River Bollin in Cheshire. **Opposite:** Alan Titchmarsh in the Picture Gallery of the house at Attingham Park, Shropshire, during the filming of *Secrets of the National Trust*.

Attingham Park, Shropshire

Attingham Park is all you'd expect of an English country house and estate. A sweeping drive through a fashionably designed landscape leads to a soaring Neo-classical façade of almost impossibly slender columns – like architectural exclamation marks. This announces itself as the house of a man who had made it in the world, certainly in this corner of Shropshire. As befitting the estate of a gentleman of such lofty achievement, it has its very own deer park and, providing accompaniments to the venison, a large walled garden. Little surprise, then, that this is the most-visited National Trust house in the Midlands.

For 160 years, Attingham was home to five generations of the same family. The mansion was commissioned by Noel Hill in 1782 – a time of booming industry and international trade. Two years later, Hill was awarded the title of Baron Berwick for supporting Prime Minister William Pitt the Younger on his East India Act, which brought the East India Company's rule in India under the control of the British Government.

The architect George Steuart designed the new house around an existing one and the layout consisted of masculine and feminine wings. In the grounds of his vast estate Lord Berwick commissioned the usual array of buildings – a stable block, a toll house, a home farm,

Opposite: Attingham Hall seen from the east, with the orangery on the right.
Above right: The working kitchen at Attingham Hall, where a committed team of staff and volunteers continue to create Georgian dishes from produce grown in the Walled Garden.
Right: Attingham has a rare Regency bee house displaying traditional straw skeps.

an orangery, an ice-house – that, together with the Walled Garden, ensured complete self-sufficiency.

Noel and his wife Anne had six children and may have married for love. The theme of love runs through the feminine side of the house. most notably in the Boudoir, which was painted *c*.1785.

Noel's eldest son, Thomas, inherited Attingham in 1789 before the house was fully complete. The 2nd Lord Berwick had his father's eye for beautiful design and making a statement. As a bachelor he completed the Grand Tour (the educational rite of passage or 'gap year' for the sons of the fabulously wealthy) and acquired very many beautiful and expensive works of art.

In 1812 he married Sophia Dobochet, a noted courtesan (her sister, Harriette, even more so, with clients including the Prince of Wales, the Lord Chancellor and four future prime ministers). His choice of wife may have surprised society, but this did not stop Lord Berwick from furnishing her apartments in an extravagant style.

The 2nd Lord Berwick's rooms in the west wing are boldly decorated; they are functional, such as the Dining Room, or say something about a man's character, such as the Library. Lady Berwick would have served tea to her guests in the stunning Sultana Room with Regency silk drapery, or entertained them by playing the harp in the Drawing Room.

Lord Berwick's most ambitious project, the Picture Gallery, was never entirely successful. It was commissioned from the Regency period's finest architect John Nash. However, it ran into problems from the beginning. Its cast-iron and glazed roof allowed more than light to flood into the gallery below, and it took until 2013 and the installation of a new roof by the National Trust to fix the persistent leak.

Opposite above: The soft and feminine Boudoir was painted for Anne, wife of the 1st Lord Berwick

Opposite below: The exquisitely delicate details on the wall and mantelpiece in the Boudoir.

Right: Close view of the dining table with elegant metalwork and period food details.

Below: Lord Berwick's Dining Room makes a powerfully masculine statement with its red walls, and portrait of William Pitt the Younger looking down from above the fireplace.

Lord Berwick's lavish spending left him near bankrupt, and he was forced to sell the contents of the house in 1827. Successive members of the family could not afford to keep Attingham functioning at such a grand level. When the 8th Lord and Lady Berwick came to live at Attingham in the 1920s, they reluctantly sold some of the 8,000-acre (3,237-hectare) estate to keep the core part intact. Their love of and care for the house and its contents was reflected in Lord Berwick's generous gift of Attingham to the National Trust upon his death in 1947.

And it is a showstopper. It is a glorious example of the country house and estate, but it is also something of a lesson of living within one's means. The Walled Garden today is a hugely popular attraction. The idea of plot to plate is not a new one, and to see how the production of fruit and vegetables operated on a country-house scale in the eighteenth century is a thing of wonder. The glasshouses were artfully controlled microclimates, with north-facing walls heated by boilers, capable of producing grapes, melons and even pineapples all year round.

Sadly, along with the rest of the estate, all this expensive ingenuity fell into neglect and disrepair, and the Walled Garden was out of production by the late twentieth century. However, regeneration is something Attingham is familiar with, and the restoration of the Walled Garden is as impressive as that of the mansion. Staff and volunteers spent nearly ten years bringing it back to life and into full production. Now the Walled Garden supplies not only produce for the tea room and shop but also flowers for the house.

Attingham Park is just one example of a country-house estate that had care and wealth lavished upon it, only to fall into disrepair when fortunes waned. Happily, its glories have been restored for all to enjoy.

Left: View down the Picture Gallery showing the impressive curved glazed roof.
Above: Tulips blooming in front of the glasshouses in the Walled Garden. Exotic fruit such as pineapples were once grown in the pinery.

NATURE, AS MAN INTENDED

The Midlands has at times been the scene of heavy industry. In this way it can fairly be described as the country's beating heartland. But every beating heart needs its lungs. While great tracts of land were built on or put under the plough to feed the country's rapidly growing population, some of the wealthiest members of eighteenth-century society spent huge fortunes on keeping swathes of their country estates as 'natural' as possible. The man they turned to was landscape designer Lancelot 'Capability' Brown, whose first and last major projects were in the Midlands, at Croome in Worcestershire and Berrington in Herefordshire. He designed in excess of 170 parks in between; here are six of Brown's best.

Stowe, Buckinghamshire

Lancelot Brown was born in Northumberland in 1716. It's not known when he became known as 'Capability', but the reason for the nickname was apparently because he would tell his clients that their property had 'capability' for improvement. In his mid-twenties, after an apprenticeship as a kitchen gardener at Kirkharle

Hall, Northumberland, he ventured south and found work as under-gardener at Stowe under William Kent, one of the founders of the new English style of landscape garden. However, Kent's protégé went on to far exceed his master.

Brown was Stowe's head gardener from 1742 to 1750. He made Stowe and Stowe was the making of him. Brown created an impression of naturalness – rolling expanses of grass, artfully scattered trees and shrubs, reflected in the glassy surfaces of sinuous lakes. To add to the Arcadian scene – the sort seen as a backdrop to a Renaissance painting full of frolicking gods, goddesses and satyrs – Brown designed buildings and statues. Stowe is full of classical allusion, with features such as the Grecian Valley, the Corinthian Arch and the Palladian Bridge.

Croome, Worcestershire

In 1751 Brown was commissioned by Lord Coventry at Croome. Before Brown, the parkland was an unproductive and unremarkable marshland with

Opposite: View across the Octagon Lake towards the Lake Pavilions and Corinthian Arch at Stowe.
Right: Croome Court on the banks of the artificial river created in the park.
Below: The west front of Petworth, seen from over the serpentine lake.

formal gardens close to the house. The marsh was drained by the installation of a system of brick-built drains, which fed into a new lake and river. Then it was out with the formal gardens and in with sweeping riverside carriage drives, clusters of trees, topped off with temples and follies. Brown wasn't only a shaper of landscapes; he also knew his plants. Croome's plant and tree collection was greatly admired, and in the 1801 *Annals of Agriculture* was described as 'second only to Kew' for its botanical diversity.

Petworth, West Sussex

One of Brown's grandest designs, Petworth is 700 acres (284 hectares) of pastoral perfection. However, it took four commissions over the 1750s to create the impression of such naturalness, requiring the removal of a formal garden complete with rampart terraces and parterres. In their place swathes of grass stretch to the horizon and border a mighty serpentine lake, all overlooked by the mansion framed by trees. It is a work of art in itself, and was painted by arguably one of our greatest landscape artists, J. M. W. Turner, in the early nineteenth century.

Wallington, Northumberland

In the 1760s the local-boy-made-good returned to Northumberland. Brown had been familiar with the rolling farmland of the Wallington estate as a child, located as it is just 2 miles (3.2km) away from Kirkharle, his birthplace, and on his route to school in the estate village of Cambo. It's interesting to think that this landscape influenced Brown's naturalistic ideas. However, as he was only too adept at proving to his clients, nature can be improved upon. At Wallington, Brown gave advice about relocating the Walled Garden in 1760 from one part of the East Wood to its present location, and he may have had a hand in designing the Owl House that now overlooks the garden. Further afield on the Estate, Brown designed new pleasure grounds at Rothley – five original drawings lay out his designs for the 'Low Lake', a causeway and an associated house.

Wimpole Estate, Cambridgeshire

At what was surely his peak, Brown designed the most idyllic landscape at Wimpole. In the 1760s–70s Brown transformed the featureless farmland into a park wrapped up in a woodland belt, with carriage rides past strategically planted trees that first concealed and then revealed perfectly framed views. The high point of a tour of Wimpole Estate was, and still is, the sham ruined castle – a picturesque Gothic folly.

Berrington Hall, Herefordshire

In what was Brown's final landscape before his death in 1783, we have the culmination of an extraordinary career and a remarkable example of not only Brown's designs but also his foresight. Only now, some 200 years later, has the landscape of mature oak and beech trees become what Brown intended. Berrington is almost a checklist of his signature and most successful features: there's a serpentine lake, ha-ha, grand sweeping drive and woodland belt. All of which makes a landscape that certainly has capabilities.

Opposite: View across the landscape towards Paine's Bridge at Wallington.
Above: The Gothic Tower on the Wimpole Estate.
Right: Berrington Hall seen within Capability Brown's parkland.

Biddulph Grange Garden, Staffordshire

The Midlands offers the garden lover a huge variety, each place with its own history and character. However, it is hard to imagine one as individual as Biddulph Grange Garden near Stoke-on-Trent. Built with a fortune made in coal and steel, it is another showpiece and is a statement of one man's religious and scientific interests, which is full of surprises and eccentricities.

It was developed in the 1840s by James Bateman, who had inherited a fortune from his industrialist grandfather. Bateman's passions were less about industry and making money and more about plant collecting and showcasing his treasures in high Victorian style. The picturesque, naturalistic parks of 'Capability' Brown, where planting was used to enhance the scene, were by this time out of fashion. Instead, the fashionable Victorian gardener wanted the setting to enhance the display of plants, most of them exotic specimens never seen before, collected by plant hunters such as George Forrest, Joseph Hooker and Robert Fortune. These men risked their lives collecting rhododendrons from Tibet and lilies from China, like horticultural Indiana Joneses. Bateman collected all of these plants – rhododendrons and azaleas being his particular favourites – and became an expert on the orchids of Guatemala and Mexico.

Left: Rhododendrons and azaleas beside the pool in the Rhododendron Ground at Biddulph Grange.
Opposite: Long, buttressed yew hedges make up the Dahlia Walk, which provides a dazzling display of colour during the summer months.

So Bateman, with help from his friend Edward William Cooke, designed a garden of compartments, each with a distinct theme, focusing on a particular species or an exotic corner of the world. The Dahlia Walk is a blaze of colour in the summer but the architecture of its hedges is a sight to behold at any time of year. There's an area entirely given over to the rhododendrons of which Bateman was so fond, and you can even experience a Himalayan Glen. Hidden behind walls of hedges and rock banks are still more wonders. Turn a corner and you can journey to China, stepping into something you might have seen on a well-known dinner service, with ornate bridge and drooping golden larch reflected in the surface of a water garden. (Indeed, Thomas Minton had been producing this design at his pottery just down the road in Stoke-on-Trent since 1798.) You'll find dragons on the parterre and fabulous fretwork in the temple, and presiding over it all is a golden water buffalo. Egypt is every bit as bold a statement, with statues designed by the sculptor Benjamin Waterhouse Hawking, and topiary pyramid guarded by sphinxes, in which the god Thoth resides. The Egyptians regarded this ape-like divinity as the author of science, religion, philosophy and magic, and indeed you'll find a curious combination of all of these at Biddulph.

Which brings us to perhaps Biddulph's most intriguing feature. The garden is quite magical, something of a gardener's paradise, each area an expression of Bateman's imagination and scientific interest as each compartment has its own microclimate. He was clearly fascinated by nature, and studied his specimens rigorously, corresponding with great thinkers of the day, including the great Charles Darwin and Professor

Right: Bridge over the pool in the China area at Biddulph Grange.

Left: Detail of a dragon on the roof of the temple in the China area.
Below right: The dragon parterre in the China area.
Bottom: Two sphinxes guard the entrance to the Egypt area at Biddulph Grange.

Opposite: The Geological Gallery is the original Victorian entrance into the garden. It is the only one of its kind, organised into bays according to the days of the Creation.
Right: Detail of Day VI of the Geological Gallery. Replica fossils have been added to the bays and the gallery has been restored to its former glory.

Richard Owen, who established the National History Museum in London. However, whereas Darwin was a man of science and empirical thought, Bateman drew on the theories of the geologist and theologian Hugh Miller to reconcile the conflicting claims of how the world was created. Bateman built the Geological Gallery, which is the only one of its kind in the world. It is a remarkable and unique exposition of earth science and religious belief.

Bateman opened the gallery to the public in 1862 to convince visitors that the geological strata and fossil finds that had recently been dug up and studied, throwing new light on to old beliefs, could still be explained in the context of the Christian story of the creation of life. Bateman's hugely ambitious work was a gallery about 100ft (30m) long, displaying a selection of rock samples and fossils set into the wall and separated into bays numbered according to the days of the Creation. The rock strata are laid out according to geologist William Smith's geological strata identification, which is still relevant today. The first couple of bays contain the granites and slates, before passing on to the limestones, sandstones and coal formations. The bay that represents the third day of the Creation features mostly fossilised plants, such as ferns. After the plant fossils come animals, and in Day VI a large turtle fossil was originally displayed.

The gallery lost many of its fossils over time and with changing owners. Fortunately these have been replaced with replicas based on contemporary records and include a juvenile ichthyosaur.

Biddulph Grange Garden is certainly a puzzling place. The winding paths through dense and tall hedges, through tunnels and around rock banks, are like a maze or the cross-section of a brain – Bateman's brain and his particular view of the world.

MONUMENTS OF INDUSTRY

The Industrial Revolution had an enormous impact on the country, providing a living wage for many and untold wealth for a few. It radically transformed the countryside. Buildings sprang up, grinding corn, spinning cotton, sharpening tools and plumbing the earth for its riches. The National Trust now looks after 49 of these monuments to industry, including the following outstanding examples.

Quarry Bank, Cheshire

As one of the best preserved cotton mills in the country, Quarry Bank gives a ready sense of what life was like for the people who worked here. The site includes a five-storey mill, three working steam engines and what is now Europe's most powerful working water-wheel, weaving sheds, workers' accommodation, and the Apprentice House, were the child workers lived.

Finch Foundry, Devon

Finch Foundry in the village of Sticklepath near Okehampton is the last working, water-powered forge in England. At its productive peak in the nineteenth century, the power of the foundry's three thundering water-wheels was harnessed to hammer, shape and sharpen around 400 tools a day. Now a romantic survival of a bygone age, it was a big business in the area, employing as many as 25 men, including blacksmiths, carpenters, wheelwrights, farriers and general workers.

Houghton Mill, Cambridgeshire

Mills were once a vital part of every community, grinding the wheat to make the flour to bake the bread. Now they nourish us with the tranquility of their riverside settings. Houghton Mill is a particularly pretty example. Set in an idyllic village location on an island on the River Great Ouse, Houghton Mill has inspired artists and photographers for generations. So loved by locals, when it came close to being demolished, it was saved and restored to working order.

Left: Quarry Bank on the River Bollin.
Opposite above: Tools on a bench at Finch Foundry.
Opposite below: Houghton Mill on the Great Ouse River.

Wellbrook Beetling Mill, County Tyrone

Beetling is the pounding of linen or cotton to give it a smooth finish. Wellbrook Beetling Mill is the last working water-powered beetling mill in Northern Ireland, dating to the nineteenth century when the country was the world's leading producer of linen. Today the thundering beetling engines give some idea of just how big that business was, contrasting with the peaceful setting on the banks of the Ballinderry River.

Dolaucothi Gold Mines, Carmarthenshire

Not all industry began with the Industrial Revolution and at Dolaucothi Gold Mines you'll find evidence of mining by the Romans 2,000 years ago. Welsh gold is famous the world over but it is found only in the Dolgellau gold belt in north-west Wales, as well as at this site. After centuries of dereliction, there were attempts to find new seams in the 1930s and remains of that operation – a crushing mill and a mine yard – can be explored today.

Levant Mine and Beam Engine, Cornwall

Levant Mine and Beam Engine is located within the St Just Mining District, one of the oldest and most densely mined areas in Cornwall. Copper and tin have been mined here since prehistoric times. The great steam-powered beam engine – still running today and such an amazing sight – was once used to pump water out of the mine, and extended out under the sea bed for over a mile. The work underground for the miners (men and boys) was hard and dangerous. The work above ground for the Balmaidens (women and girls) was equally tough. By 1836 Levant employed 320 men, 44 women and 186 children, some as young as seven years old. On the afternoon of 20 October 1919 a great disaster occurred when the man engine (which carried the men up and down the shaft) broke and 31 miners fell to their deaths. The man engine was not replaced and the lowest levels of the mine were abandoned. The mine closed in 1930.

Top: Wellbrook Beetling Mill.
Above: Mine buildings and track at Dolaucothi Gold Mines.
Opposite: The surface remains of Levant Mine, including stacks and beam engine houses.

THE NORTH

Those whose taste runs to wilder fare should head a little further north, since there are few places more remote to explore in the Lake District than Wasdale. The breathtakingly beautiful valley is home to Wastwater, England's deepest lake, with its dramatic screes sweeping down from the top of Illgill Head to the lake below, causing ever-changing reflections to appear on the lake's surface.

It's also the setting of England's highest mountain, Scafell Pike (3,208ft/978m). When British rock climbing was in its infancy in the late nineteenth and early twentieth centuries, Wasdale was at the centre of the scene. Today, 'the birthplace of British mountaineering' remains a popular starting point for climbers tackling Scafell Pike.

On the other side of Scafell, Langdale, in the centre of the Lake District, is popular with hikers, climbers and fell-runners alike, all drawn to the surrounding hills and the beautiful, mirror-like lakes. The area is best known for its brooding surrounding mountains, the Langdale Pikes (peaks). Langdale consists of two valleys: the larger Great Langdale was glacially formed, while the smaller Little Langdale, also glacial, is what is known as a hanging valley – a smaller, tributary valley set higher than its main valley.

After a day out in the Langdales, the best place to relax is the National Trust-owned-and-run pub, Sticklebarn. All of Sticklebarn's proceeds help us look after the Langdale region. The pub is a welcoming building of slate, stone and timber, with panoramic views of the Pikes, and has served generations of Langdale farmers. It has plans to become one of the Trust's most environmentally progressive buildings, powered by a hydroelectric plant harnessing the water tumbling down Stickle Ghyll from the tarn behind the pub.

Opposite: Sticklebarn tavern, a great spot to unwind after a day's walking, while sharing stories around the fire pit on the terrace.
Above: Dawn over the Langdale valley. A landscape carved by glaciers has more recently been shaped by farming, with the valley floor dissected into fields by stone walls.

WATERFALLS

There's something about water dropping off the edge of a cliff that stirs something almost magical in the human soul. Waterfalls have inspired myths, legends and artistic passions for centuries. They've also powered British industry and in doing so have changed its landscapes forever. In the summer they can dazzle with their rainbow beauty, but in winter, swollen by rains and brooding beneath steely skies, they are at their dramatic, elemental best.

Lydford Gorge, Devon

The pretty River Lyd, meandering through its steep-sided, oak-clad valley on the western side of Dartmoor, has carved some dramatic features out of its granite valley. The stars are the 98ft (30m) White Lady Waterfall, which falls like a skein of silken hair down the rock face, and the turbulent pothole evocatively known as the Devil's Cauldron. During the seventeenth century Lydford Gorge was the hideout of the Gubbins family, a large band of sheep-stealing outlaws. By the nineteenth century, it had become a favourite spot on the routes of Victorian tourists unable to tour continental Europe during the war against Napoleon.

Aberdulais, Neath, Neath and Port Talbot

The Dulais is a flash-flood river, so its levels rise and fall very rapidly. People recognised its potential for power-generation as early as 1584, when Aberdulais Falls were used to provide energy to Britain's first copper works, where copper was manufactured from ore imported from Cornwall. Since then, they've also powered corn-milling and a tin-plate works. The current weir and waterfall were added during the nineteenth century, and the wheel in place today is made from steel. At 27ft (8.2m), it is the largest electricity-generating water-wheel in Europe, with 72 buckets that rotate at a rate of five revolutions per minute.

Today the falls are among the most accessible waterfalls in Wales, with managed gravel paths, and lift access provided to enable viewing for wheelchair users from the top of the waterfall platform, providing a spectacular place from which to see this natural wonder.

Buttermere, Cumbria

Of all the beautiful waterfalls of the Lake District, Buttermere has the greatest variety. In wintertime, every insignificant gulley and channel in the landscape is transformed into a tiny, talkative mini-fall, gurgling and chattering through the landscape. At the other end of the scale is Sourmilk Gill, which tumbles down nearly 1,300ft (396m) of steep fellside from Bleaberry Tarn to Buttermere. Sourmilk Gill brought huge pink boulders crashing down from Red Pike during the floods of 2009. There's also Scale Force, an hour's walk from Buttermere village. It falls almost 170ft (52m), making it the largest single drop in the Lake District, and it's

Opposite: Steps through Lydford Gorge.
Below: Aberdulais Falls.
Right: Sourmilk Gill, Buttermere.

hidden away in a narrow rock gorge above Crummock Water. Meanwhile, Holme Force is a beautiful series of falls cascading from mossy rock arches, evocatively named the Grey Mare's Tail by locals.

Henrhyd Falls, Brecon Beacons, Powys

The highest waterfall in south Wales (90ft/27m) plunges into a wooded sandstone gorge in Graigllech Wood. With the nearby Nant Llech Valley, the shady, damp surroundings of the area make for a wildlife haven. Tree warblers and wrens live in the trees, which are mostly sessile oak and ash, and dippers and wagtails search for insects along the river. There is a smaller waterfall further down the river, where leaping trout have been spotted. Henrhyd is at its best after a heavy downpour.

Falls of Glomach, Ross-shire

Glomach means 'gloomy', and these Highland falls are often enveloped in mist, but it adds to, rather than detracts from, their drama and atmosphere. The National Trust for Scotland has looked after the Falls since 1944. Visitors prepared to make the effort to hike the 12-mile (19.3km) round trip through the glorious mountain scenery to reach them are well rewarded. A clamber up the slippery rocks reveals the spectacle of the water tumbling in a single 370ft (113m) drop into a rocky cleft. Glomach is among the highest waterfalls in the country.

Grey Mare's Tail, Dumfries and Galloway

Grey Mare's Tail is what's known as a hanging valley waterfall near Moffat in southern Scotland. It forms as the Tail Burn flows from Loch Skeen in the upper valley into Moffat Water Valley below. Together with the surrounding Grey Mare's Tail Nature Reserve, it is home to many rare plants and habitats. If you're lucky you might spot a peregrine falcon here, or the herd of hairy mountain goats that roam the area. There is evidence of Iron-Age settlement in the form of Tail Burn Fort.

Opposite: Henryhd Falls.
Above: Falls of Glomach.
Right: Grey Mare's Tail Falls.

The Yorkshire Dales

Leaving the Lake District behind and travelling 45 minutes or so to the south east leads to another wild region with a completely different character – the Yorkshire Dales. Like the Lakes, the landscape of the Dales has been shaped by both humans and nature. Stone villages and traditional farming landscapes, ancient woodlands, former mine workings and spectacular waterfalls are set in valleys (dales) topped by purple, heather-clad moorland.

There are some wonderful abbeys and castles to poke around, too, including the ruins of Fountains Abbey near Ripon, North Yorkshire.

This is primarily a limestone landscape, with some striking geological features that include 'pavements' – flat, horizontal slabs of carboniferous limestone called clints, separated by grikes, the vertical cracks between the slabs. Pavements are another remnant of the last ice age. They are created by water exploiting cracks, fissures and joints in the exposed limestone slabs, thereby creating the clints and grikes that give them the appearance of paving slabs. Now, thousands of years later, there are complex patterns in the pavements. The contrasting habitats of the deep, sheltered grikes and the flat, sunny clints make for a great diversity of species, including rare ferns and flowers with evocative names such as hart's tongue fern, bloody cranesbill and common rockrose.

Opposite above: Alan walks through the ruins of Fountains Abbey, North Yorkshire, during the filming of the series *Secrets of the National Trust*.
Opposite below: Traditional dry-stone walling and field barn at Wharfedale, North Yorkshire.
Above: The limestone escarpment at Malham Cove, Yorkshire Dales National Park, shows the distinctive 'pavement', created by water exploiting cracks and fissures on the rock's surface.

Traversing from north to south, Wharfedale is one of the longest and most beautiful valleys in the Yorkshire Dales. The National Trust owns a large slice in the form of the Upper Wharfedale estate, which has pretty drystone walls and wildflower meadows, caves to explore and waterfalls to discover. Yockenthwaite is a lovely place to admire the scenery and amble along the river, poking into pools along the way. Spare a thought for the Tour de France peloton, which in 2014 passed through this area during Stage One, powering up the 1,460ft (445m) climb along Kidstones Pass above Cray.

To the west of Wharfedale lies the Malham Tarn Estate. It's a National Nature Reserve with walking and cycling routes, and views across the limestone pavements. At its heart is Malham Tarn, the highest freshwater lake in England.

Lucky visitors to Malham Tarn might just catch a glimpse of one of Britain's most endangered mammals – the water vole. The Trust's rangers have recently reintroduced around 200 of these charismatic little creatures into the Tarn. They were wiped out here in the 1960s – probably, ecologists think, by mink released from nearby fur farms. Water voles are common in the rest of Europe but they remain Britain's fastest declining wild mammal, having disappeared from almost 90 per cent of rivers and streams.

The water vole was the inspiration for Ratty, hero of Kenneth Grahame's *Wind in the Willows* (1908). Literary nostalgia aside, water voles have a vital part to play as part of the Trust's major new vision for land management in the Yorkshire Dales. They will graze areas of the riverbanks, creating space for rare plants to grow, and over time will colonise the rivers and streams surrounding the Tarn. They will also provide a food source for struggling predators, including barn owls and otters. Rangers will continue to monitor the health of the population over the coming years.

Above: The River Wharfe meanders through the valley at Yockenthwaite, Upper Wharfedale.
Opposite: Janet's Foss on the Malham Tarn Estate is a popular destination for a walk from Malham village.

The East Coast

No chapter on the wild places of the North is complete without turning to the region's stunning and dramatic coastline. These are the edges of our country at its most raw and elemental, sometimes scarred by an industrial past, sometimes home to rare wildlife, and always great fun to explore. England being what it is, jolly seaside towns intersperse the drama.

On the Yorkshire stretch, the Trust looks after the coastline from Filey to Saltburn – an area with plenty of military history, including Ravenscar Chain Home Low Radar Station. It was constructed as part of a coastal defence system in 1941 on a cliff top just south of the village of Ravenscar, near Scarborough, an area known as Bent Rigg.

The radar station was in use until after the Second World War. Four brick buildings remain: a transmitter/receiver block, a fuel store, an engine house and a communications hut with a barrel-shaped corrugated roof. The footings of a complex of about 12 barrack blocks and other domestic buildings can also be seen in the corner of the field, although it takes a little more imagination to visualise them as they once were.

After the end of the war, the buildings fell into disrepair. For a time it seemed they might be demolished, but in 2000 they were surveyed by a volunteer and a National Trust consultant archaeologist. Both the radar buildings and the remains of the barrack complex were given Scheduled Monument status by English Heritage in 2002.

Other highlights of this stretch of coastline include the village of Port Mulgrave, a mining settlement 9 miles (14.5km) north-west of Whitby. The old ironstone mine entrance remains, some 50ft (15m) above the high-water mark. There's also Cowbar Nab, which in springtime is home to a raucous colony of gulls, kittiwakes, fulmars and the occasional razorbill, and a Trust-owned field at Runswick Bay, which contains two reservoirs built to feed an ironwork's blast furnace in the mid-nineteenth century. The remains of that furnace are at the base of the slumped sea cliffs. The reservoirs are now managed as wildlife ponds, the deeper of which houses all three

Left: The derelict buildings of the Ravenscar Chain Home Low Radar Station are perched on the cliff top. **Opposite:** View from the cliffs above the Loftus Alum Works, a large quarry complex on the North Yorkshire coast.

of Britain's native species of newt, including the rare great crested newt.

Further north, the wild expanse of the Northumberland coast opens up. From Druridge Bay to Lindisfarne, there are wide skies and blue seas, pretty fishing villages and

over 30 miles of beaches, many with excellent rock pools. Seals, dolphins, wading shore birds and nesting terns call this place home – especially at Long Nanny.

Long Nanny Tern site is a nationally important breeding site for terns. The Trust has been protecting it since

Left: The Farne Islands are home to a thriving puffin population, with some 40,000 pairs nesting each year. **Opposite:** The Farne Islands lie 1–3 nautical miles off the Northumberland coast. The resistant igneous dolerite outcrops form strong columns, which give the islands and stacks their steep vertical cliffs.

1977. For nine months of each year, the site blends into Beadnell Bay, a vast stretch of unspoilt beach, but in early May, thousands of birds arrive for the start of the three-month breeding season. The main three ground-nesting species are the little tern, Arctic tern and ringed plover. During nesting time, National Trust rangers live on site, camping on the dunes to provide 24-hour protection for the birds from predators and welcoming visitors to the site. In 1977, just three pairs of little terns visited Long Nanny. Now, 30–50 pairs use the site each year.

A natural highlight like no other is the Farne Islands. It's no exaggeration to say this is truly one of the UK's most impressive wildlife spectacles. During the summer breeding season the islands are home to 23 species of nesting sea-bird, including thousands of puffins, Arctic terns and guillemots, all adding raucous voices in a cacophony of sound.

Every few years, Trust rangers carry out a census of the islands' population of puffins as an indication of the overall health of the bird populations. The most recent, which took place in 2013, showed there were almost 40,000 nesting pairs on the islands.

There are 28 Farne islands, many of which are submerged at high tide, and the National Trust looks after them all. They are divided into two groups: the Inner Group and the Outer Group. Despite their remoteness, some of the islands are habitable. Today, rangers live on Inner Farne for nine months of the year and Brownsman for three months, welcoming visitors and protecting and monitoring the nesting bird life, but over the centuries hermits, monks, lighthouse-keepers, soldiers and even shipwrecked sailors have all called these islands home.

The best known is St Cuthbert, a seventh-century hermit who became one of the most important medieval saints

Richard the Younger, unwittingly sold it to an agent of Sir Francis Drake, who made further modifications.

Anglesey Abbey, Cambridgeshire

A twelfth-century priory converted to a country house in the fifteenth century, Anglesey Abbey was the country home of the Fairhavens. It is particularly known for its landscaped gardens, laid out in the 1930s in an eighteenth-century style by the estate's last private owner, the 1st Lord Fairhaven, and for the family's fabulous collection of furniture and *objets d'art*.

The West Coast

Britain's north-western coastline has quite a different feel to its north-eastern counterpart. While the tourist hubs of Blackpool and Morecambe are just what you'd expect from resort beaches, move outside them and the coast is dramatic and beautiful, the remnants of our industrial heritage as much a part of the landscape here as the windswept beaches.

Formby, just outside Liverpool, is a case in point. You can clearly see the offshore wind farms from its sandy beach, but their unapologetic presence adds to both the views and the area's sense of history. Formby's coastline is continually changing today as is has for millennia, its dunes sculpted and re-sculpted by the ever-present wind. The dunes are a valuable habitat for rare wildlife and also act as sea defences for the town of Formby. Pine woodlands behind them house a substantial number of red squirrels.

Formby has the dubious honour of being the fastest eroding coastline in National Trust ownership. On average, 13ft (4m) of dune is lost annually to the waves. Some experts put it down to climate change. Others point out that the coast here has always been dynamic, its geomorphology alternating between erosion and accretion over thousands of years. Still others note that in the early twentieth century the River Mersey was widened and deepened, which affected the direction of the prevailing waves, causing them to strike Formby's coastline from a new angle.

Left: Pine woodland behind the beach at Formby, Merseyside.
Opposite above: The ruins of St Patrick's chapel at Heysham Head, Lancashire. The graves cut directly into the rock are in the foreground.
Opposite below: Sunset over the beach at Formby.

Whatever the reason, the capricious waves have revealed a precious gift. Not far from the beach is Formby Point, part of the Sefton Coast Site of Special Scientific Interest, one of the largest complexes of sand flats and dunes in the UK – and the location of hundreds of prehistoric footprints. Seven thousand years ago, rising sea levels had isolated Britain from Europe and this part of the Sefton coastline shifted back and forth in the ensuing period. By about 4500BC people were visiting the area regularly, and the footprints of those travellers and wild animals have been preserved in the intertidal mud.

Archaeologists from the Trust and Liverpool museums have been studying the footprints and have come to some fascinating conclusions. They have discovered, for instance, that the average height of the men was 5ft 5in (1.66m) and of the women was 4ft 9in (1.45m). The women and children collected shells and looked for nesting birds, while the men were often accompanied by footprints of the red deer they'd been hunting. Radiocarbon dating sets the dates of the footprints' creation at between 5,100 and 3,400 years ago, from the late Neolithic to the middle Bronze Age. The footprints are as ephemeral as the coastline. Visitors will discover some newly exposed by a tide, hinting at the lives of those people as they ran and walked and even played in the mud. Then, two or three tides later, they'll be gone, erased as though they were never there but, thankfully, still preserved, this time in the form of photographs.

Just south of Morecambe, the Trust looks after the sandstone grassland and peaceful woodland that makes up the Heysham coast. One of the highlights here is St Patrick's Chapel, a small Anglo-Saxon ruin on the headland close to the village of Heysham. The chapel is notable for eight graves cut into the rock itself in the graveyard. Some have straight sides, others are curved to fit the shapes of bodies. One in particular is small and perhaps held the body of a child. They all have socket-holes cut

into the rock that probably once held timber crosses. The chances are that the people buried in these graves were of high status, singled out as they were to be laid to rest in rock rather than directly into the ground.

Further north again you'll find Sandscale Haws National Nature Reserve, a vast and beautiful dune habitat

that's home to a wonderful variety of rare species. Six of Britain's native species of amphibian live here, including the rare natterjack toad. Natterjacks are Europe's noisiest amphibians, and their distinctive croaks echo through the evening air during their breeding season in April–June. The different amphibians have subtly different habitat requirements,

Your first thoughts of Scotland might lead you to the Highlands. Certainly the glens are an iconic sight, their raw beauty conveying some of the indomitable Caledonian spirit.

But, as with everywhere else in these long-inhabited isles, true wilderness if hard to find. The rugged beauty of Glencoe in the Highlands is something to experience, with its misty mountain tops, windswept moors and brooding atmosphere. It is these qualities which make its peaks appealing to walkers, its vistas so perfect for visitors and its scenery ready to shine on the cinema screen. The National Trust for Scotland cares for this most famous of Scottish glens, ensuring its special qualities are not lost.

The many islands off the coast of Scotland also offer abundant adventure and opportunities to get close to nature. Once the often arduous voyages have been made, the rewards are views of incredible beauty and memories that will last forever.

As well as coast and country, the National Trust for Scotland looks after many historic houses, gardens, castles, even an entire town. Everywhere there is fascinating evidence of how people of the past have worked with the raw materials of nature to shape the world around them.

Previous pages: View from Port an Eorna on the Balmacara Estate, Ross-shire.
Opposite: Culross on the Firth of Forth in Fife is an authentic example of a burgh of the seventeenth and eighteenth centuries.

Glencoe and Dalness, The Highlands

Glencoe is easily the most famous glen in Scotland. Its scenery is simply breathtaking, and if you have the heart and lungs for it, there are eight Munros (mountains of 3,000ft/915m and more) to climb.

It is climbers we have to thank for this gift, this wild and spectacular scenery, as the land was purchased by the National Trust for Scotland in the 1930s using money donated by the Scottish Mountaineering Club. Its chair at the time, Percy Unna, had certain stipulations that the landscape should not be 'tamed'. He was strongly opposed to facilities such as cable cars and mountaintop restaurants that he'd seen in Europe, and didn't want what he saw as intrusions built in Glencoe.

This is one of the reasons that Glencoe exists largely in its primal state, and indeed being in Glencoe feels like being at the dawn of time. Maybe it's because of the quality of the air, the clarity of the streams, the almost total absence of buildings and human habitation, but the place feels newly formed.

Yet its dramatic peaks and valleys, forged by fire and shaped by ice, are unquestionably and unfathomably ancient. Glencoe is the remains of a supervolcano, which erupted about 420 million years ago. During the last ice age, around 11,700 years ago, glaciers carved out the U-shaped glen.

This ancient landscape offers many modern attractions. Climbers and hill walkers have a huge variety to choose from, and there is skiing in the winter. At the heights these people aspire to they might see a golden eagle, as Glencoe includes a Special Protection Area for these magnificent birds.

Left: The untamed landscape of Glencoe appears undisturbed by human activity.

ISLAND LIFE

The British Isles are made up of hundreds of islands, 194 of which are permanently inhabited. Scotland has 97 of these, although some have populations in single figures. On every one of these islands, the wildlife far outnumbers the human occupants, but all have to adapt to their particular insular life.

Fair Isle, Shetland

Far-flung Fair Isle sits halfway between Orkney and Shetland, and is one of Britain's most remote inhabited islands. It is well named, being as beautiful as it is small – only 3 miles (4.8km) long and 1½ miles (2.4km) wide. This crofting community has developed a thriving traditional crafts industry, building boats, spinning, weaving and, of course, knitting, for which the island is world famous. Twitchers are as well catered for here as knitters, the island being internationally renowned for its birds and in particular its sea-bird colonies.

Iona, Hebrides

As small as Fair Isle, Iona similarly has a reputation that far exceeds its size. Today visitors are drawn to its white sandy beaches, clear turquoise waters and abundant wildlife, but people have been coming here to soak up its special spiritual atmosphere since the sixth century. It was from a monastery on this island, founded by St Columba and his followers in AD563, that the Gospel of Christ spread across Scotland.

St Kilda World Heritage Site, Western Isles

It's hard to believe that St Kilda, part of an extinct volcano and the remotest point of the British Isles, was ever inhabited. The community that lived here until 1930 survived by catching gannets, fulmars and puffins for food, feathers and oil, as well as farming certain crops. When the last islanders accepted their way of life was no longer sustainable, St Kilda was bought by the Marquess of Bute, who managed it as a bird reserve before bequeathing it to the National Trust for Scotland in 1956. The only world heritage site in that is recognised for both natural and cultural importance, it remains an important breeding station in north-west Europe, home to gannets, puffins, and Manx shearwater.

Opposite: St Martin's Cross, a Celtic cross from the eighth century, stands next to the abbey on Iona.
Above: Fair Isle South Lighthouse.
Right: Abandoned cottages on the main street of Village Bay, St Kilda.

be shipped in and by planting a shelter belt of thousands of pines to protect the garden from the harsh elements. He was helped in creating a unique microclimate at this latitude by Inverewe's position, which benefits from the warm currents of the Gulf Stream.

What Osgood created is today regarded as one of the most beautiful gardens in Scotland. It is also noted for having the most northerly planting of rare Wollemi pines. These were only known through fossil records until a living species was discovered in 1994 growing in a temperate rainforest gorge in New South Wales. Now they grow in the Highlands! This is the achievement of the small but dedicated gardening team that now looks after Inverewe, but it was only possible due to the work of Osgood, and his daughter Mairi who gifted the garden and 2,000-acre (809-hectare) estate to the National Trust for Scotland just before her death in 1952.

Crathes Castle, Garden and Estate, Aberdeenshire

Crathes Castle, with its turrets and towers overlooking formal gardens to woodland and countryside beyond, rises up like something out of a fairy tale. What was here before, once upon a time, was something very different. The Burnett family was made a gift of land by Robert the Bruce in 1323 for services to the King. You can only imagine how perilous the Middle Ages must have been for the family to decide to build a fortress of timbers on an island in the middle of a bog on the estate.

It evidently kept them safe, as it was the same family that built this castle in the middle of the sixteenth century. However, due to political unrest in the reign of Mary, Queen of Scots, the castle wasn't completed until 1596. The next century appears to have been a more settled time for the Burnett family, and some remarkable

decoration survives from that period. In several Jacobean rooms there are original Renaissance painted ceilings of a distinctive style found in Scotland, where the decoration is painted straight on to the boards and joists of the floor of the room above.

The Burnetts continued to flourish – perhaps a little too well – and an additional wing was built towards the end of the seventeenth century to accommodate the 3rd Baronet of Leys' 21 children. (Sadly this wing was destroyed by a fire in 1966.)

The gardens, too, were developed and haven't stopped evolving since. The Walled Garden and its topiary are around 400 years old, with some of the sculpted British yews dating to 1702. Sitting within, and taking shelter from, these aged walls is something altogether more modern. Divided into eight garden rooms by those veteran yews, the 4-acre (1.6-hectare) Walled Garden follows the early twentieth-century Arts and Crafts tradition of themed planting in herbaceous borders, including the Blue and Pink border and the famous June Borders, and also the later additions of the Golden and Red Gardens. These were the creations of Sir James Burnett, the 13th Baronet of Leys, who gave Crathes to the National Trust for Scotland in 1951.

Left: Crathes Castle stands six storeys high and has an elaborate turreted top floor. The clock was added in Victorian times. Inside, the castle is famous for its painted ceilings, which adorn many of the rooms.

Above: The kitchen garden at Trengwainton with its west-facing sloping beds.
Left: View through the entrance of the Walled Garden to one of the glasshouses, Wimpole Estate.
Opposite: The Pineapple at Dunmore Park.

NORTHERN
IRELAND

Northern Ireland has a huge amount to offer visitors and an impressive variety of attractions. The people here are generous with their welcome, and often ready with a story or several.

Perhaps Northern Ireland's best-known attraction, the Giant's Causeway, was forged in the fires of erupting volcanoes at the end of the Cretaceous period, when dinosaurs literally roamed the Earth. Whichever story about its creation you believe, it is a must-see spectacle of the natural world.

Over 60 million years later, the landscape has settled down into some glorious wildernesses, where the wildlife is wonderfully abundant. The loughs and rivers, the mountains and uplands – even the bogs – boast a heartening diversity of animal and plant species.

Contrasting with the untamed parts of the country are manicured parks and gardens, as well as achingly beautiful architectural creations. Some very wealthy people commissioned some extraordinarily elegant things, which can now be enjoyed by all rather than a privileged few.

The giants may be consigned to folklore, but there is a wealth of opportunity for exploration, with any number of stories to be made up along the way.

Previous pages: The Mourne Mountains from Murlough National Nature Reserve, County Down. The range is the highest in Northern Ireland, with Slieve Donard the tallest peak at 2,800ft (854m).
Opposite: Drowned drumlins at Strangford Lough, a large shallow sea lough in County Down.

Giant's Causeway, Country Antrim

The Giant's Causeway has a big name and a big reputation to live up to. It is the stuff of legends and folklore, and locals have been creating stories about it for countless generations. The most familiar rocks are those on the Grand Causeway, tens of thousands of hexagonal columns forming an uneven, and very slippery, pavement stretching out to sea towards Scotland. This curious sight inspired the tale most associated with the Causeway, often told but it's a good one so bears repeating.

Finn MacCool was a giant who, for the most part, lived a quiet life with his family here on the coast of Northern Ireland. But there were rivals, other giants, and perhaps to pre-empt a challenge from his Scottish neighbour, Benandonner, Finn laid down the gauntlet and built the Causeway so they could meet to join battle. However, on his way across to Scotland, Finn spied Benandonner in the distance and realised that his rival was much bigger, taller and stronger than he had appeared from across the water. Finn decided he didn't want to fight Benandonner anymore and ran back home as fast as he could. Finn found his wife Oonagh and explained the terrible mistake he had made. Oonagh, being the brains of the pair, devised the plan of dressing Finn up as a baby and putting him into their son Oisín's cot, covering him with blankets and wrapping a shawl around his head. Just then there was a loud banging at the door – Benandonner! 'Where's Finn?' he demanded, 'I want to fight him!'

Right: Steeped in myth and legend, the Giant's Causeway is a natural wonder. Its importance was recognised in 1986 when it was designated a World Heritage Site by UNESCO.

'Calm down!' said Oonagh, 'Finn's out herding the cows. Why don't you come and wait for him and I'll make you a cup of tea?' So Benandonner had his cup of tea but then grew impatient again. 'Where's Finn?' he roared. Oonagh explained again, 'He is out herding the cows but while you're here why don't you let me introduce you to our son Oisín?' When Benandonner saw the giant baby in the cot he got scared. He thought, if that's the size of the baby, how big is the father? Benandonner immediately ran out of the house and home across the Causeway, tearing it behind him to make sure Finn couldn't follow. The other end of the Giant's Causeway still exists today on the island of Staffa (see page 100).

That's one version of events. The various scientists who've been studying this formation over the last 350 years or so have come up with their own interpretations: some believed the columns were formed in fire and by volcanic events; others believed they were formed by minerals crystallising underwater. Now it's generally agreed that the basalt pillars are the result of lava flows that began around 60 million years ago when the North American tectonic plate began to split from the Eurasian plate. A series of eruptions with rapid cooling in between caused cracks to appear in the solidified lava. The action of wind and wave also helped to form the landscape, creating standout features such as the Camel. Not in fact a dromedary, nor for that matter a Bactrian, it is actually a a dolerite dyke, formed from cooling lava that pushed its way up through layers of softer rock, which wore away over hundreds of thousands of years to leave a camel-shaped outcrop.

However, the fiction can often be more entertaining than fact, and the guides at the Causeway today, continuing a long tradition of entertaining as well as informing, have a virtually inexhaustible supply of stories; possibly one for each column of the Grand Causeway.

Above: Horizontal contraction in cooling magma created the characteristic basalt columns that make up the Causeway.
Opposite: The rope bridge to Carrick-a-Rede is suspended 98ft (30m) above the sea. A walk across is not for the faint-hearted.

Carrick-a-Rede, County Antrim

While Carrick-a-Rede might not have the global reputation of its near neighbour, the Giant's Causeway, it offers the thrill-seeker an experience few other National Trust places can match. People come to test their nerve on a rope footbridge, an updated and much sturdier version than the one that fishermen would throw each year, across the 65ft (20m) wide chasm between the mainland and the island, 98ft (30m) above crashing waves.

Nearly 300 years ago, when fishermen noticed that Carrick-a-Rede (which translates as 'The Rock in the Road') caused migrating Atlantic salmon to be diverted from their path around the island, past a point where the fishermen could set their nets, they thought the rewards worth the risk. Those early bridges, flung across the gap at the start of each fishing season, were very basic with a single handrail only. Crossings were made dozens of times a day by men, women and children laden with

baskets of fish, from March to September. It was one of the most successful fisheries on the Antrim coast, with catches of up to 300 salmon a day common until the 1960s. By 2002, due to the intensification of fishing out at sea as well as pollution in the rivers where the fish spawn, 300 were caught over the whole season and the fishery was eventually forced to close.

However, since coming into the care of the National Trust in the 1960s, Carrick-a-Rede has found new life and has a different sort of attraction. The views from the coastal path and island itself are glorious, and from May to late July you can observe at close quarters a large and raucous colony of sea-birds. The crossing continues to reward those that dare.

Castle Coole, County Fermanagh

We've walked in giants' footsteps and dared to cross dizzying chasms but, such is the diversity of what Northern Ireland has to offer, we come now to experience the stately grandeur of eighteenth-century high society.

Castle Coole is one of Ireland's finest Neo-classical houses. As you approach the meticulously symmetrical and elegant façade – an Ionic portico flanked by Doric colonnaded wings – there is no doubt that its creator, the 1st Earl of Belmore, intended to impress. What is

Opposite: Sunset over the coastline at Carrick-a-Rede, County Antrim.
Below: The south façade of Castle Coole, seen from across Lough Coole.

perhaps more surprising is that it was only ever intended to be a summer retreat. Lord Belmore was a political heavyweight and heir to a huge fortune accumulated through commerce. So when he came to build his castle, no expense was spared – an estimated cost of £57,000 in 1798, equivalent to approximately £20 million today – and he engaged the leading Georgian architect, James Wyatt. Wyatt was also responsible for the interiors and designed some of the most important furniture in the mansion. It is rare to see architect-designed Neo-classical pieces in the very place for which they were crafted, and it is staggering to think of the wealth that made this possible. The fine plasterwork friezes and ceilings by master plasterer Joseph Rose are truly the icing on the cake.

And yet there is more to explore. Wandering through the corridors and rooms of the basement complex gives an idea of just how many people were needed to lay on the lavish entertaining hosted by the Earls of Belmore. Then there is the estate, 1,200 acres (490 hectares) of wooded parkland, grazed by cattle and sheep as originally intended. Not so much how the other half lived, but perhaps the top two per cent.

Above right: The colonnaded entrance of Castle Coole.
Right: Detail of gilded 'Grecian' couch *c*.1816, supplied by the Dublin upholsterer John Preston for Castle Coole.
Opposite: The Formal Garden from the Dodo Terrace at Mount Stewart, County Down. The terrace is decorated with plinths and statues of dodos and other creatures.

Mount Stewart, County Down

Where Castle Coole is perhaps the acme of architecture, Mount Stewart is gardening on a grand scale. It was still about showing off one's wealth, taste and refinement, but done with horticulture rather than bricks and mortar.

The designer of this globally celebrated garden was the Lady Londonderry, an influential interwar socialite. When her husband succeeded to the Marquessate in 1915, Edith took it upon herself to transform what were a rather plain house and grounds.

She was aided by the garden's position on the edge of Strangford Lough (see page 124), in a south-west facing natural amphitheatre, which means it enjoys a climate that is unusually mild for these parts. This allowed Edith's imagination to run riot and to experiment with a variety of planting, producing a series of formal gardens, each with a distinct character.

Edith's own personality is evident in the garden. Edith the socialite also went by the name of Circe, seducer of Odysseus, and in the various gardens she created – the

Shamrock Garden, the Sunken Garden, the Spanish Garden, the Italian Garden and the Dodo Terrace to name a few – there is drama, classical mythology and Irish folklore. But it isn't all for show. Her scholarly knowledge of garden history combined with her passion for plants, their form, colour and scent, to produce what you see today.

She had help – her head gardener Thomas Bolas trained at Chatsworth, and she had a horticultural mentor, Sir Herbert Maxwell, who said to her: 'The lust for lilies is a contagious disease as deadly as Rhododendronitis, from which you suffer incurably already' – but the overarching design was hers. In Homer's *Odyssey*, Circe is described as living in a mansion that stands in the middle of a clearing in a dense wood. Naturally, one of Edith's creations was her own Lily Wood, a piece of woodland that formed a shelter belt around the garden.

With all the money, time, intellect and imagination Edith had at her disposal, the result is something truly sublime, one of the world's greatest gardens.

Left: The Spanish Garden at Mount Stewart with the house behind. The microclimate of Mount Stewart situated near Strangford Lough allowed Edith to bring a Mediterranean influence to her garden designs.

REMARKABLE TREES

It's often said that when you're looking too closely at something, you can't see the wood for the trees. It's true – if you've ever enjoyed a wander through any of the woods, gardens and parks looked after by the Trust, you may not have stopped to pay much attention to the individual trees (unless, of course, you're a keen climber of them!). Well, it would be a shame to miss them, so here to enjoy some of the limelight are the biggest and best.

The Mother of All
At Florence Court near Enniskillen in County Fermanagh you'll find an ancient Irish yew, bearing some signs of age, which is hardly surprising, as she's had a *lot* of offspring. Planted here in about 1767, she is the tree from which all Irish yews around the world are descended.

Widest Girth
Florence Court is home to another champion tree: it's a common lime but of uncommon size. Its girth – the distance around the trunk – measures 424in (1,078cm) and the tree is still growing.

Tallest Tree
The tallest tree towering above all the others at 190ft (58m) is a grand fir, which you'll find (just look up) in Skelghyll Woods near Ambleside in the Lake District. The Trust's, and in fact England's, tallest grand fir is all the more remarkable for growing to such height on an exposed ridge above Windermere.

Oldest of All
Another venerable yew in the care of the Trust, known as the Ankerwycke Yew, is thought to be around 2,500 years old. It grows near Runnymede, Surrey, and would have been standing when King John put his seal to the Magna Carta there in 1215.

SAFETY IN NUMBERS

Nature can be precarious at times. Changes in habitat, climate, availability of food and breeding sites, all these things can threaten the survival of species. It's all too easy to think of examples where populations have suffered, often at the hand of humankind. But here are a few success stories, of survival in droves, to remind us of the wealth of wildlife out there, provided we invest in it.

Strangford Lough, County Down
From the Norse meaning 'strong fjord', Strangford Lough is the biggest sea inlet in the British Isles. Covering 60 sq miles (150 sq km), the lough has a multitude of habitats, including roughly 100 islands along with many islets, bays, coves, headlands and mudflats. Naturally, this place of outstanding, unspoilt beauty attracts more than weekend kayakers. It's a winter destination, a getaway from the Arctic circle, for many migratory birds, and one species in particular flocks here in hundreds of thousands. Up to 90 per cent of the global population of light-bellied brent geese from Artic Canada arrive at Strangford Lough each Autumn – up to 38,000 birds.

Brownsea Island, Dorset
The largest of eight islands in desirable Poole Harbour, covered in woodland rich in pine and oak, Brownsea Island is an exclusive resort indeed. If you're a red squirrel, that is. The island has been deliberately kept free of its American cousin, the grey squirrel, so Brownsea is one of the few places you'll find a thriving population of reds. They are smaller than greys and timid of humans; your best chances of spotting one is in autumn.

Farne Islands, Northumberland
The Farne Islands, a cluster of 15–20 rocky islands depending on the tide, might not seem the most hospitable and supportive habitat but there is wildlife

here in raucous abundance. There are ducks – shelducks, mallards and eider ducks; terns of the Arctic, roseate, sandwich and common varieties; herring gulls, great black-headed gulls and lesser black-backed gulls; fulmars, cormorants and shags; razorbills and kittiwakes; and let's not forget the guillemots. But of all the Farnes' feathered friends, perhaps it is the puffin that pleases most. Around 37,000 pairs of these pint-

sized birds breed here. Counting so many puffins could leave our rangers quite breathless.

Blakeney National Nature Reserve, Norfolk

At the heart of the Norfolk Coast Area of Outstanding Natural Beauty, on the north coast enjoying huge views out to sea, Blakeney Point has become home to the largest grey seal colony in England with over 2,000 pups

Left: Brent geese over Strangford Lough.
Top: Puffins on Staple Island, Inner Farne.
Above: Red squirrel on Brownsea Island.

born each winter. These pups are the colour of snow when new, and don't turn grey until they've tripled in size, outgrowing their white babygrows. So successful is the colony at Blakeney Point that the mortality rate among pups is as low as five per cent.

Stackpole, Pembrokeshire

Stackpole boasts not one but two success stories. Both species were once very rare, but they are now doing rather well in the rich and protected environment around the Bosherston Lakes. Otters are utterly adorable to watch and at Stackpole they've started to come out to play. Once shy and secretive, now that they enjoy protection and numbers are up, their antics are much more visible, particularly around the lakes and on the bridges. Less photogenic perhaps, but just as valued, are greater horseshoe bats, which are here in greater numbers than anywhere else in Wales. The way they hunt for prey depends on continuous cover from trees

and hedgerows, so it's heartening to know they have got this at Stackpole.

Sandscale Haws National Nature Reserve, Cumbria

The natterjack toad (*Epidalea calamita*) is a calamitous toad indeed and one of three protected amphibians in the UK, primarily due to habitat loss. They are now almost entirely confined to coastal areas, and even there in small numbers, so the loud and distinctive croak that gives them their name comes in useful for finding a mate. Approximately a quarter of the UK's estimated population of 4,000 natterjack toads are found at Sandscale Haws, where they are carefully monitored. Around 20 spawning pools, which in a wet year can add up to around 49 acres (20 hectares), are surveyed each spring. The time taken to do this has so far been rewarded with data that shows the population is stable.

Opposite left: One of the otters on the Stackpole Estate.
Opposite right: Natterjack toadlets in shallow water at Sandscale Haws National Nature Reserve.
Above: A grey seal on the sand dunes at Blakeney National Nature Reserve.

WALES

banished Nefydd and named the lake after his son. Even the birds of the air were so saddened by the death of the beautiful young prince that to this day, so the story goes, they do not fly across the water of Llyn Idwal.

Walkers descending from the cwm can look out for the Devil's Kitchen, a 'black hole' in the back wall that often has sinister clouds of 'steam' cascading from its depths. It is said to tempt weary travellers in to eat and rest, but once in the Devil's Kitchen they are never be seen again. In fact, the 'steam' is merely moist Atlantic air coming in from the south-west, which condenses as it rises up the Eastern slopes of Nant Peris over Rhos Llyn y Cŵn, forming clouds. This walk also offers a wonderful view of Llyn Ogwen, a lake, with a National Trust ranger base and information point that's said to be the very lake

of Arthurian legend where Excalibur was flung and, apparently, remains to this day.

Ysbyty Ifan, Conwy

North of Snowdonia in Conwy, close to the town of Betws y Coed, is the small village of Ysbyty Ifan. It looks sleepy now, but in bygone days it had a reputation for offering sanctuary to robbers, bandits and highwaymen.

The Ysbyty Ifan Estate is immense, consisting of over 19,768 acres (8,000 hectares) of moorland, river valleys and hill farms. The village used to be called Dôl Gynwal (Gynwal's meadow) but it was renamed 'Hospital of St John' in 1190 after a religious order, the Knights of St

John, set up a hospital and hostel here. The village is on the path of many of the old pilgrim routes through Wales, and the Knights considered themselves duty-bound to care for any passing pilgrims on religious journeys and on their way to the Holy Land.

The Knights had the privilege of sanctuary. During the Glyndŵr uprising of 1400–15 against the English, they extended this sanctuary to some of the most famous Welsh bandits and rebels of the time. Sir John Wynn of Gwydir, writing at the end of the sixteenth century, called it 'a receptacle for thieves and murderers'. The King experienced such dreadful weather during his attempts to quell Owain Glyndŵr and his rebels that some said he could bend the very forces of nature to his will.

The hospital and hostel were abolished during Henry VIII's Dissolution of the Monasteries. The Knights had also built a church, which became the parish church for the area. Although that building has gone, there are artefacts from it in the current church, including an effigy

of Rhys ap Maredudd, who recruited Welsh soldiers to help Henry Tudor defeat Richard III during the Wars of the Roses. Henry was born in Pembroke Castle and the Welsh thought he was *Y Mab Darogan*, a foretold son who would rise up and lead the Welsh to defeat the English. Some poets insist it was Rhys ap Maredudd who killed Richard III at Bosworth in 1485, but this is impossible to prove.

Powis, Powys

Unlike many castles built by the English to quell the Welsh, Powis belonged to the Welsh prince Owain ap Gruffydd ap Gwenwynwyn. It remained in his family from 1286 until 1578, when it was sold to the Herbert family. The Herberts spent the next 400 years filling it with fabulous items ranging from sumptuous fabrics to a gold and jewelled tiger's head finial.

In 1784 Lady Henrietta Herbert, daughter of Lord Powis, married Edward Clive, eldest son of Major

General Robert Clive, also known as Clive of India. He was Commander-in-Chief of British India and secured a great tract of what is now Bangladesh, South India and Pakistan for the British Crown, amassing a huge personal fortune in the process. Their marriage joined the Powis and Clive estates, and Clive's fortune funded vital repairs at Powis. Today Powis houses the Clive Museum, which contains the UK's largest private collection of Indian treasures. The formal Baroque garden is also world-renowned.

Powis has a few ghosts associated with it, including a lady dressed in black who is said to sit beside the fireplace in the Duke's Room, and the sounds of a piano that apparently can be heard drifting from the Ballroom Wing when it is empty and the doors locked. But its spookiest story concerns a man in the gold-laced suit. It's uncertain exactly when the following is supposed to have happened, but the man is said have visited an old lady who was staying at the castle. On the third night he led her to a small room and showed her a chest hidden beneath a floorboard and a key tucked into a wall crevice. He told her that if she sent both to the Earl of Powis, who was in London, he would stop haunting the castle. Whether the Earl was happiest with the gift or the promise is unclear, but he is said to have thanked the woman and arranged for her care for the rest of her life.

Opposite: Powis Castle has a series of Italianate terraces leading down to the gardens. It is one of the greatest surviving examples of Baroque garden design in Britain.
Above: The view from the terrace of Powis Castle over the lower gardens and out over the surrounding countryside.

CASTLES

Moats, battlements, knights and towers – what's not to love about exploring a castle? Even when reduced to ruins, their imposing façades bring out the inner child in young and old alike. All the castles in Trust care have stories to tell and many have played their part in Britain's history for hundreds of years.

Bodiam, East Sussex

When you say 'castle', this is probably the kind of place most people have in their minds, with a wide moat, battlements, spiral staircases and towers with wondrous views. It was built in the fourteenth century by Sir Edward Dallingridge, a knight of Edward II's realm, who ensured the comfort of his family's living quarters by including a total of 33 fireplaces in the design. They would have sat and listened to stories by candlelight.

Chirk, Wrexham

Chirk is the last of the Welsh castles from the reign of Edward I still inhabited today. It was built between 1295 and around 1310 as part of a chain of fortifications along the border to keep the Welsh subdued under English rule. In the years that followed it swung between glory and despair, gifted to noblemen by the king and then taken away from them again in disgrace. From the late sixteenth century it became home to the Myddelton family and was lavishly furnished. It has a medieval fortress and a dungeon. Schoolchildren in particular love to feel the weight of armour and watch demonstrations of medieval-style weaponry.

Dunster Castle, Somerset

The fine walls of Dunster Castle rise above the pretty medieval village of the same name, surrounded by woodland and gorgeous gardens. It was owned by the Luttrell family for over 600 years, during which time

Above: Chirk Castle in the pink early morning light.
Opposite: Bodiam Castle, surrounded by its impressive moat.

Left: The Rock Garden at Sizergh.
Above: Falkland Palace and Garden.
Opposite: Dunster Castle.

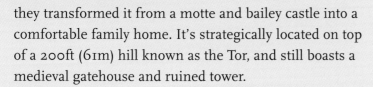

century, but by the mid-1500s James IV and James V had turned it into a royal palace. It was a favourite retreat of the Stuart monarchs, who hunted and practised falconry in the woodlands that surrounded it. Falkland Palace is also notable for its 'real tennis' court, which was built in 1539 and is still in use today. (Real tennis is the game from which modern lawn tennis derived.)

Sizergh, Cumbria
Sizergh is the medieval family home of the Strickland family, who have been here since 1289 and are still in residence. Lady Strickland is related to the second husband of Catherine Parr, sixth wife of Henry VIII. The garden has a glorious rock garden planted to change colours through the seasons, and the 1,600-acre (647-hectare) estate, which includes some important wetland and woodland, was included into the Lake District National Park when its boundaries were extended in 2016.

they transformed it from a motte and bailey castle into a comfortable family home. It's strategically located on top of a 200ft (61m) hill known as the Tor, and still boasts a medieval gatehouse and ruined tower.

Falkland Palace, Fife
This grand castle is situated in beautiful calm gardens in the midst of the village of Falkland. It was owned by the MacDuff clan – the Earls of Fife – in the thirteenth

Llyn Cwm Llwch, Brecon Beacons, Powys

From dragons and war to an enchanted fairy island. Llyn Cwm Llwch is a small glacial lake tucked behind the nearby peaks of Pen y Fan and Corn Du. It is beautifully clear. It's a pleasant surprise to discover the lake among the highest of the Brecon Beacon peaks while out hiking. Perhaps its very unexpectedness has contributed to the legends of the May Day fairies that surround it.

The story goes that hidden by enchantment in the middle of the glacial lake is a beautiful island garden inhabited by extremely courteous and hospitable fairies. Every May Day, a secret passage used to open up from a rock to the island. The fairies loved to entertain guests. Those people brave enough to pass through the passage to the fairy garden were plied with fruit and flowers, entertained with magical music, and even offered glimpses into the future. But, as ever with these tales, there has to be a catch – that nothing must be removed from the island. Inevitably, one May Day a greedy visitor secreted a flower in his pocket. As he emerged from the rock, the flower vanished, he lost all his senses, and from that day to this, the rock door has never opened again.

Skirrid, Black Mountains, Brecon Beacons, Monmouthshire

Skirrid, the Sacred Hill, Holy Mountain – all these names belong to the 1,594ft (486m) hill on the eastern side of the Black Mountains in the Brecon Beacons. A smaller hill, Little Skirrid, trails along behind it a couple of miles to the south.

Skirrid is also known as Ysgryd Fawr. *Ysgryd* is a beautiful Welsh word meaning something that has shivered or been shattered, and this word really does describe the hill's shape most evocatively. The top commands glorious views of Sugar Loaf mountain, one of the highest peaks in the Black Mountains and also in National Trust care.

Skirrid is formed from red sandstone and has a jagged edge along its western side caused by landslips during the Ice Age. There are some fabulous legends attached to it, one of which declares that part of the mountain broke off at the very moment that Jesus was crucified. Walkers braving the climb will find the remains of a ruined Catholic chapel to explore on its summit. The Chapel of St Michael's was used during the Reformation, and services were held here until at least 1680.

Before that, however, legend tells of a character called Jack O'Kent who liked to engage in intellectual and physical sparring matches with the Devil. For instance, it is Jack who is said to have tricked the Devil in that old folktale about crops: if Jack planted and tended the crops, the Devil would ensure the rain and sun came to help them grow. The Devil said he wished to receive the top part of the harvest, but Jack planted turnips, so at harvest time the Devil was thwarted. Furious, the following season he said he wanted the 'butts', or bottoms, of the crop, but this time the crafty Jack planted wheat.

Jack is variously described as a wizard, a cleric and occasionally a giant, and legends about him are used to explain much of the geological lie of the land, particularly around Herefordshire and Monmouthshire. In the story about Skirrid, Jack is a giant who argued with the Devil over which was bigger, Sugar Loaf mountain some 5 miles (8km) to the west, or the Malvern Hills across the border in England. Jack said Sugar Loaf; the Devil said the Malverns. When Jack proved the Devil wrong, the Devil tried to make the Malverns higher by carrying extra soil across and dumping it on top of them. But his carrier broke on the way there, and the extra soil fell on to Sugar Loaf instead, making it still higher.

The cleft on the edge of Skirrid is apparently the result of Jack's heel landing in it as he leapt across from Skirrid to Sugar Loaf. There's a nearby rock known as the Devil's Table, where the Devil is said to have sat and supped as Jack leapt across. Look for it from the landslide – it's shaped like a toadstool.

There's also a story, which some say is about Skirrid and others say is about Trelleck Beacon 25 miles (40km) or so distant. This time Jack was in a throwing competition with the Devil; the result was the three standing stones still visible at Trelleck.

Opposite: Skirrid stands in isolation, separated from the rest of the Black Mountains by the Gavenny Valley. The photograph is taken from Sugar Loaf.

Worms Head, Gower, Swansea

Worms Head snakes out into the sea at the southern end of the spectacular Rhossili Bay on the South Gower. Its name comes from the Norse word *Wurme*, meaning 'dragon' or 'serpent'. While the Vikings established settlements and kingdoms in England, they never took control of Wales nor subdued the Welsh kings, but they did settle in parts of West Wales, including Gower. It's likely that Worms Head took its name from one of their legends. The invaders are said to have thought of the rock as a sleeping dragon, partly because of its shape and partly because in stormy weather a blowhole on the north side makes dramatic booming noises, throwing spray into the air like steam from a dragon's nostrils.

At just a mile (1.6km) long, Worms Head is the most westerly point on Gower. It becomes an island at high tide, but is otherwise linked by a rock causeway to the mainland at low tide. The causeway is only exposed for a few short hours each day, so walkers should time their expedition carefully and be sure to check tide tables, or risk being trapped for half a day until the tide turns once again. Those who do miscalculate, however, are in good company. An unwary Dylan Thomas once fell asleep and missed his chance to get back until the next low tide, an experience he relates in 'Who Do You Wish Was With Us?' (from *Portrait of the Artist as a Young Dog,* 1940). He wrote:

> I stayed on that Worm from dusk to midnight, sitting on that top grass, frightened to go further in because of the rats and because of things I am ashamed to be frightened of. Then the tips of the reef began to poke out of the water and, perilously, I climbed along them to the shore.

Apparently, Thomas briefly considered moving to Rhossili, near Worms Head, but changed his mind upon learning the nearest pub was 5 miles (8km) away. A fine little legend on which to end this chapter!

Opposite: This view of Worms Head shows the distinctive shape of the sleeping dragon.
Left: A sweeping view of the sandy beach at Rhossili Bay from the south.

Cemlyn and North Anglesey Coast

Walks along the North Anglesey coast take you along headlands and rocky small bays that show off the rugged beautiful coastline at its best. A highlight is Cemlyn Bay, where a brackish lagoon is separated from the sea by a shingle ridge. It's an important habitat for sea-birds, particularly the tern colony that has made its home at the western end, which includes the only breeding colony of Sandwich terns in Wales.

White Cliffs of Dover, Kent

The White Cliffs have been a symbol of homecoming and hope for generations. Walking up top gives an unparalleled view of the busy English Channel, while around you rare wildlife, especially flowers, grasses and invertebrates, thrive on the chalk-grassland habitat. Inevitably, there's plenty of military history here, especially at Fan Bay Deep Shelter, a labyrinth of Second World War tunnels that the National Trust has restored and opened to the public. Take a torchlit tour and find out about the lives of the soldiers who lived here while they worked the gun battery above.

White Park Bay, County Antrim

White Park Bay formed between 200 and 50 million years ago. Fossils are still regularly found on its white sandy beach, especially ammonites and belemnites. At certain times of day dolphins and porpoises can be seen playing off the coast, while sea-birds dive for fish and fly overhead. This is the site of one of the first Neolithic settlements in Ireland, and the remains are still here to be explored. The ancient sand dunes are home to plenty of rare species of butterfly and moth.

Opposite above: The White Cliffs of Dover, from St Margaret's Bay.
Opposite below: Cemlyn Bay, with the lagoon to the left of the shingle bank.
Left: Chalk arches at White Park Bay.

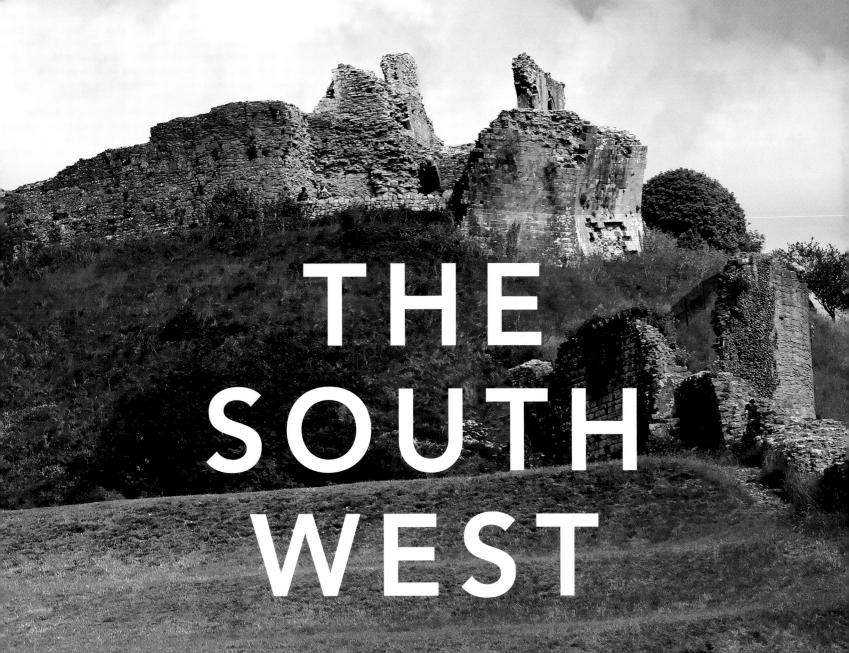

THE SOUTH WEST

The theme for this chapter can be interpreted in many intriguing ways, and the South West has National Trust places that embody them all. Layers in time are visible in the most literal sense if you take a stroll anywhere along its beautiful coastline. Dinosaurs once roamed this landscape. The cliffs, landslides and beaches were formed by rocks first laid down and then exposed by the elements over the past 250 million years. It has transformed from desert to swamp to deep tropical seas, before settling into today's familiar landscape where holidaymakers picnic and walk. Even now, the elements continue to sculpt it in a reminder that nothing in this world remains in stasis.

Thousands, rather than millions of years ago, Neolithic and Bronze-Age folk were going to almost unimaginable effort to create enduring monuments to their faith at Stonehenge and Avebury in Wiltshire. The landscape tells the story of a civilisation that depended upon the sun for its very survival and went to extraordinary lengths to ensure its reappearance each year.

Mere centuries are just a blip in Britain's history in comparison, but there are political layers and implications even at this timescale. From the Norman Conquest via the Civil War to twentieth-century political upheavals, National Trust properties have been affected by those who called them 'home'. Each person has left an impression, however faint, on their building's history.

Previous pages: The Keep of Corfe Castle, Dorset.
Opposite: The sandstone cliffs at Burton Bradstock, Dorset, comprise alternating layers of harder and softer sands laid down towards the end of the Jurassic period.

Jurassic Coast, South Devon and Dorset

The Jurassic Coast is the name given to the 95-mile (153km) stretch of coastline between Exmouth in East Devon and Studland in Dorset. It is a stunning part of the country. The sea has carved the sandstones, clays, limestones and chalks into magnificent shapes, leaving stacks and arches, rich sandy beaches, coves and unexpected caves. The colours and textures are magnificent – sticky clays and smooth pebbles, deep reds and oranges ranging through blues and greys, greens and browns, black and white. The Jurassic Coast is home to rare wildlife and plants, and this stretch of the coastline was added to the World Heritage List in 2001 and is beloved of walkers and birdwatchers alike.

The rocks and fossils found here date from the Mesozoic Era – the time spanning the Triassic (252–201 million years ago), Jurassic (201–145 million years ago) and Cretaceous (145–66 million years ago) periods. This was a time when dinosaurs ruled the world. During the Triassic, the land was arid desert. As time passed, rising sea levels produced first a low and swampy landscape, then submerged most of the South Coast as they rose to more than 656ft (200m) higher than today. The Mesozoic Era was brought to an end 66 million years ago by the mass extinction event that wiped out the dinosaurs and heralded the rise of mammals as the world's dominant species.

The coastline changes in nature from west to east as the rocks of different geological periods are exposed. The red mudstone and sandstone cliffs of East Devon formed in the Triassic deserts. It is rare to find fossils here. Further east, the coast around Weymouth and Portland reveals sedimentary rocks laid down towards the end of the Jurassic period, including Portland limestone, a famous building stone. Fossil-collector and palaeontologist Mary

Opposite: Handfast Point and the chalk stacks of Old Harry Rocks mark the eastern end of the Jurassic Coast.
Above: The pebble beach at Ringstead Bay with the chalk cliff of White Nothe in the background. A walk to White Nothe offers a fantastic view towards Weymouth and the Isle of Portland.

Anning made world-famous discoveries in the cliffs around Lyme Regis, including the world's first correctly identified ichthyosaur skeleton. This stretch of coastline still yields exciting finds to amateur collectors.

Formed in coastal swamps amidst fluctuating sea levels, the rocks of the Jurassic Coast are particularly rich in marine fossils – especially prehistoric lobsters and other crustaceans, starfish and sea urchins, sharks and rays, and seashells and ammonites. The insect forebears of garden craneflies, dragonflies and grasshoppers have also been identified. Some of the rarest fossils come from early mammals – usually tiny fragments or teeth, but important parts of the evolutionary record nonetheless. Flowering plants did not appear until the early Cretaceous period, so most of the plant discoveries are conifers and ferns.

Most impressive of all are the fossils of the mighty reptiles and amphibians of this time. The Jurassic Coast is the source of some of the most important fossil finds, including ichthyosaurs, plesiosaurs and giant crocodiles and amphibians. The short stretch of Dorset coast between Charmouth and Lyme Regis is the only site where fossils of scelidosaurus have been found. Scelidosaurus was a medium-sized, armoured plant-eater and an early ancestor of better-known plated dinosaurs such as stegosaurus. Local collector David Sole found the most complete specimen as recently as 2000; subsequent discoveries of other parts from the same dinosaur have added to his find.

While you're unlikely to be as lucky as David was, there are plenty of opportunities on the Jurassic Coast for anyone who fancies trying their hand at collecting. If fossils are not picked up, the chances are high that the sea will wash them away or batter them on the rocks. It's important, however, only to collect loose fossils and never to dig or hammer into the cliff face. It's also crucial to respect that not every beach is safe to collect from and that collecting is forbidden in some places.

The National Trust looks after a third of this important coastline, including Burton Bradstock, Ringstead Bay and Old Harry Rocks. A highlight – in all senses of the word – is Golden Cap, the highest point on England's South Coast. It's a 626ft (191m) rocky outcrop between Charmouth and Bridport in Dorset, named for the pale golden-orange greensand top visible from miles around. It takes about 40 minutes to hike to the top, an effort rewarded with views from Portland Bill in one direction to Start Point in the other, and inland as far as Dartmoor.

Further east, a walk along the Purbeck coastline reveals more Cretaceous rock – limestone with its origins in swamps and lagoons, sand and grit formed in shallow seas and rivers. There are active quarries working this area today. At Keates Quarry, near Spyway, quarrymen Kevin Keates and Trevor Haysom made a very special discovery in 1997 – a watering hole at a lagoon where a group of dinosaurs once gathered to drink. More than 100 fossilised tracks are pressed into a flat layer of rock, probably made by brachiosauruses – long-necked plant-eaters that could weigh up to 50 tons. Once production had moved to a different part of the quarry, access to the footprints was opened to the public.

Opposite: Looking east along the Dorset coast to the high point of Golden Cap. Frequent landslides on the cliffs between Charmouth and Golden Cap expose more and more fossils to add to the record and our understanding of Earth's history.

Lighthouses

The National Trust has a few lighthouses in its care, but most of the lighthouses you'll see on its land and elsewhere in England, Wales and the Channel Islands are the responsibility of Trinity House, an organisation that has been in existence since Henry VIII granted it a Royal Charter in 1514 making it responsible for maritime safety. As part of this remit, Trinity House has built and operated many of Britain's lighthouses over the centuries.

South Foreland Lighthouse, Dover, Kent

A lighthouse has shone from the White Cliffs above Goodwin Sands in some form since Brother Nicholas de Legh hung a little lantern off the cliffs near his village in 1367 to warn passing ships of the dangers. Since then, it has been through several evolutions and has pioneered some modern technology, most notably in 1832, when Michael Faraday – best known for his ground-breaking work on electromagnetism – was Scientific Advisor to Trinity House. Faraday arranged for Frederick Holmes's idea of using a carbon arc lamp in South Foreland's tower to take place, making it the first lighthouse in the world to shine an electric lamp. The National Trust took it over when it was decommissioned in 1988. It has lit up just once since – in 2012, when it shone in honour of Queen Elizabeth II's Diamond Jubilee.

Souter Lighthouse, Whitburn, Sunderland, Tyne-on-Wear

Souter was the first lighthouse to be specifically designed and built to make use of alternating electric current. Despite its name, it is located a mile to the south of Souter on Lizard Point. The cliffs are higher at Lizard and it offers better visibility. The 77ft (23.5m) high lighthouse was built in 1871 and designed by James Douglass, the Victorian civil engineer best known for the fourth Eddystone lighthouse in Devon. It used the most advanced technology of its day.

Left: Souter Lighthouse and fog station.
Above: South Foreland Lighthouse.

163

Left: The 'Dutch' or parterre, a pretty formal garden on the east side of Kingston Lacy, was first laid out in 1899 and is still planted with the original scheme.

Most Haunted

At least 200 of the National Trust's properties are rumoured to be haunted. Some of the ghosts drift benignly through walls or doors, or sit reading in a library, only to disappear when approached. Some are tragic, carrying their own heads in their arms or dripping blood from wounds; others are mischievous: children closing doors and giggling, or shop stock dislodged from shelves. Whether or not you believe in ghosts, the stories undeniably add intrigue to the histories of the places they are said to inhabit.

Newton House, Carmarthenshire

Many visitors have claimed ghostly or paranormal visions or experiences at the Grade II listed former home of the Rhys (or Rice) family. They most frequently report seeing the ghost of Walter the butler in the basement, or scenting his tobacco smoke lingering in the air. Sometimes muffled voices are heard, or lights will unexpectedly dim and relight. In the main house, more sinister reports persist of throats clutched by invisible hands on the staircase.

Blickling Hall, Norfolk

Blickling was built on the site of a former home of the Boleyn family, and it's possible that Anne Boleyn, second wife of Henry VIII, was born there some time before 1505. Her white-clad ghost is said to wander the grounds and glide through the corridors on or around the anniversary of her execution on 19 May 1536. Sometimes she carries her severed head in her arms; sometimes she arrives with her head held in her lap as she sits in a coach drawn by four headless horses and driven by a headless coachman.

Opposite: A misty morning at the Blickling Estate.
Right: The wine cellar at Newton House.

Treasurer's House, York, North Yorkshire

In 1953, an apprentice heating engineer called Harry Martindale was working in the cellars of Treasurer's House when he heard the sound of a trumpet. To his astonishment, he saw a carthorse and a troop of exhausted-looking Roman soldiers in battle dress, walk through the wall and pass through the cellar. They seemed small, as they were only visible from the knees up, but they were walking with their feet below the floor – along, it was later discovered, the old Roman road that used to pass through where the house now stands. After Harry went public with his story, experts said he must have seen soldiers from 'The Forgotten Army' left behind when other garrisons were recalled.

Hughenden Manor, Buckinghamshire

Possibly the most benign Trust haunting is at Hughenden, home to Conservative Prime Minister Benjamin Disraeli. He is said to occasionally appear to guests on the stairs of his former home. Fran Penny, Visitor Operations Manager, lives at Hughenden: 'Yes, apparently Disraeli has been seen on the stairs. If you go up the stairs from the ground floor, the first half landing feels cold in the corner (personally, I think we've got a draft!). Also, one volunteer thought someone touched them on the bottom in the library, but when she turned around there was no one there, so she put that down to Disraeli too!'

Lyme, Cheshire

Sir Piers Legh, a former owner of Lyme, was killed at the Battle of Agincourt on 25 October 1415. His wife was at the funeral – but Blanche, his mistress, was not permitted to attend. She is said to have died, grief-stricken, shortly afterwards. Today, Knightslow Wood at Lyme is allegedly haunted by a ghostly funeral procession with the weeping Blanche trailing behind, dressed all in white.

Opposite: Treasurer's House, built over a Roman road.
Above: Hughenden Manor, where Disraeli's presence is still felt.
Right: Knightslow Wood at Lyme, site of a ghostly funeral procession.

185

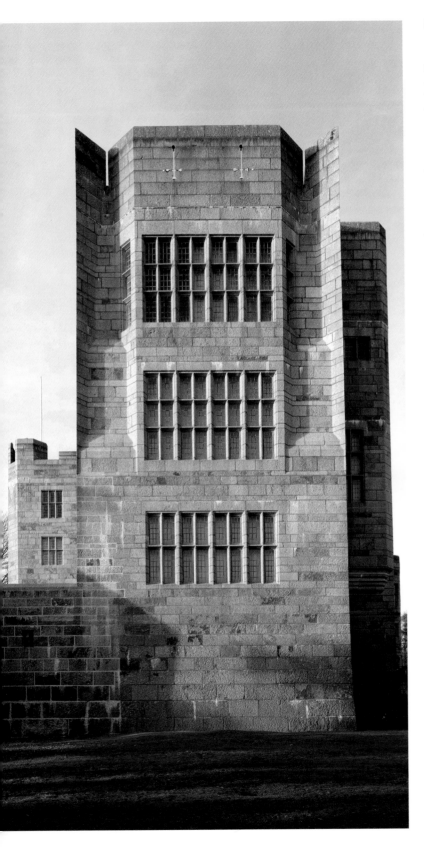

Castle Drogo, Devon

Castle Drogo was inspired by the rugged tors of Dartmoor that dominate its Devonshire setting. It is a twentieth-century castle – the last one built in England.

It was the vision of Julius Drewe, a wealthy businessman who formed the grocery company Home and Colonial Stores with a partner in London in 1883. The stores sold everything from tea to margarine and they made Drewe very rich – with enough money to retire at the age of 33.

Around this time, Drewe had begun to research his family tree. He found a connection to a Norman baron who had lived in the manor at Drewsteignton, a Devon village on the edge of Dartmoor, during the Crusades. The baron's name was Drogo de Teign, also known as Drew de Teignton. Julius believed he had a connection to this illustrious ancestor, so in 1910 he began buying up land in the area. By the time of his death in 1931 he had acquired 1,500 acres (607 hectares).

Drewe decided an ancestral castle was needed to complete the image of his distinguished history. He enlisted the services of Edwin Lutyens, the British architect behind the Viceroy's Palace in New Delhi and London's Cenotaph, to create one for him. Luytens is known for adapting traditional designs and giving them a modern twist.

Drewe briefed Lutyens to create a castle that would seem to dominate its landscape and appear a solid, confident fortification – not a pastiche. The interior would be the ultimate in comfortable modern living. The castle is constructed from locally quarried granite blocks. The design borrows heavily from the medieval and Tudor periods, the walls being up to 6ft (1.8m) thick in places, although its battlements and other defence trappings are purely decorative. Inside there is electricity throughout,

THE
SOUTH
EAST

It would be clichéd to describe the South East as the most populous region of England. Yes, it has more than its fair share of houses, but gardeners will attest that some of the greenest and most pleasant parts of our land are found attached to homes.

It would be clichéd, too, to say that the region, with its links by sea and air, is the nation's economic and financial hub. But when people earned their fortune in the city, what did they do? They built or bought a country pile. These were the palaces of the political elite, the country retreats where royals took their repose, and the houses that hosted the cream of society. However, these properties are now open for us all to enjoy, and will remain so indefinitely in the care of the National Trust.

And a thing of beauty is a joy forever. That's a cliché we can all live with.

Previous pages: The Rose Garden at Sissinghurst Castle, Kent.
Opposite: At Polesden Lacey, Surrey, the kitchen garden was transformed into a rose garden by Margaret Greville. Pergolas support Edwardian rambling roses, and the borders are filled with shrub roses, climbing roses and lavender hedges.

Fenton House and Garden, London

In one of north London's leafier suburbs, a few hundred yards up the road from Hampstead's underground station, is Fenton House and Garden. It's something of a hidden gem, buried in one of the world's most-visited cities, and indeed many overlook it. As a member of London Small Historic Houses, it isn't the grandest mansion but small can most certainly be beautiful.

It's a Georgian merchant's house, built around 1686. The merchant family who lived here in the 1730s, the Gees, lined their pockets through the sale of silks and linens. Thanks to a series of careful owners, most recently Lady Binning, who bought the property in 1936 and gave it to the National Trust in 1952, Fenton House is a showpiece of elegance and refinement, inside and out.

With all the symmetry and elegant proportions you'd expect of a Georgian house, it is rather handsome. However, it doesn't boast about its good looks, and the exterior decoration and ornamentation are typically restrained. The neo-Georgian interiors were mostly the work of Lady Binning, who filled it with family heirlooms and a variety of collections. Today it still houses some fascinating collections, including paintings by a group of English Post-Impressionist painters called the Camden Town Group, and rare examples of early keyboard instruments.

Given its location, the garden is really quite extensive. The rows of identical terraces that became such a feature of the rapidly expanding towns and cities of the Georgian period – think Edinburgh, Dublin and Bristol as well as London – attracted the very wealthy to take up residence, even with only a small square of green at the front. At Fenton House, the occupants did rather better than that.

The house is detached and overlooks a garden divided into two levels. The upper level is more formal, with a rose garden, terrace walks around a lawn and carefully clipped topiary. Steps from the rose garden down to the lower level lead you into a delightful walled area.

As well as a glasshouse and kitchen garden, there is a 300-year-old orchard, where around 30 different heritage varieties of apples and pears flourish. Here the formality of the upper level gives way to something far more relaxed. In spring, the grass is allowed to grow and the orchard is transformed into a flowery meadow. A wonderfully natural scene in the metropolis, it's not only attractive to us, but it brings in the bees and other pollinators. Come autumn, the fruits have ripened, and on Apple Day, in late September, visitors are invited to sample some of these rare and delicious apples, along with other treats such as apple-blossom honey – tastes to transport you far from the city.

Opposite: The formal garden at the back of Fenton House showing clipped topiary trees and hedges.
Above: Roses blooming at Fenton House and Garden.
Right: View over the City of London from the garden.
Following pages: The less formal appearance of the orchard and grassy meadow in summertime.

Perhaps the most famous landscape designer of all, Lancelot 'Capability' Brown, also contributed to Claremont. When Major-General Robert Clive (also known as Clive of India on account of his role in founding Britain's Indian Empire) bought Claremont in 1769, he commissioned the capable Mr Brown to build a replacement mansion and move a road. Clive was reputed to have spent over £100,000 on rebuilding the house and a complete remodelling of the already celebrated pleasure grounds, but he didn't live long enough to enjoy the results. The estate passed through a rapid succession of owners before it received a sort of royal reprieve.

In 1816 Claremont was bought by the British nation through an Act of Parliament as a wedding present for George IV's daughter Princess Charlotte and her husband Prince Leopold of Saxe-Coburg. The newlyweds loved their home – Princess Charlotte wrote regularly of her great affection for Claremont – and they added features such as the Camellia Terrace. Charlotte's cousin, the young Victoria, loved coming to play here, escaping from the suffocating environment of court, where she was being primed for her queenly duties. For the next hundred years and more, the house and landscape were much cherished and little altered. Then in 1922, the estate passed out of royal hands on account of Victoria's grandson's service for the Germans in the First World War. The inheritance was disallowed by the Government and a large part of the Claremont estate was sold for housing development, leaving 85 hectares (210 acres) of garden. By 1949, when Claremont was passed back to the nation and into the care of the National Trust, just 49 acres (20 hectares) remained.

But while the size of the landscape is diminished, its rarefied atmosphere isn't. Here you can escape from ordinary life, enjoy extraordinary views, relax like royalty or play like a princess.

Polesden Lacey, Surrey

Polesden Lacey is the epitome of an Edwardian country retreat. Its history starts long before this period – it was once the residence of the playwright Sheridan – but Mrs Greville so put her mark on the place that it transports you to the 1930s. You can almost hear the clinking cocktail glasses and tinkling laughter of bright young things.

Margaret Greville was a well-known and well-connected hostess. The daughter of brewery multi-millionaire William McEwan, she could certainly organise a gathering. When her father bought Polesden Lacey in 1906 for her and her husband Ronald, it became the venue for her celebrated house parties.

She put her heart and considerable eye for interior design into creating the perfect place in which people could relax and socialise. As sole heir to her father's fortune on his death in 1913, she could furnish her home and landscape her garden in incomparable style. She had the architects responsible for the Ritz Hotel remodel the house, with interiors ranging from the restrained Neo-classical Library to the lavish Gold Saloon, which literally glistens in the light cast by the Baccarat crystal chandelier. Old Masters hang on the wall and there are diamond-studded treasures by Cartier, not to mention Fabergé. The kitchen garden was transformed into a cut flower garden to ensure that the house was full of fresh blooms and buttonholes were always available.

Margaret loved sharing her home with her large circle of friends and acquaintances, perhaps because Ronald died a year before it was ready for them in 1909, leaving Margaret a 45-year-old widow with no children.

So Margaret filled her life and her home with beautiful things and equally glittering company. She could call a number of royalty friends, including Queen Mary, and she invited the Duke and Duchess of York (the future George VI and Queen Elizabeth) to spend part of their honeymoon here in 1923. They so enjoyed Margaret's hospitality they stayed for two weeks, the Duchess of York describing Polesden Lacey as 'a delicious house'. Margaret bequeathed Polesden Lacey to the nation upon her death in 1942, and since then the National Trust has been serving up this dish of a house. It is now one of the Trust's top ten most-visited properties. Well, we know Margaret liked to draw a crowd!

Below: The lavender walk in full bloom at the east end of the Rose Garden.

Right: The east front of Polesden Lacey, the Regency house that was transformed into a luxurious Edwardian mansion by Margaret Greville.

Below right: The Library is decorated in the Neo-classical style.

Left: Ralph Dutton designed the gardens at Hinton Ampner as a series of rooms, each with its own character. This is a tranquil view of the house across the pond.
Below: Mushroom-shaped topiary in the Sunken Garden.

Above: The Gothic summer-house at Woolbeding.

Right: The Sermon on the Mount Yew Garden at Packwood House.

Oppposite: The gardens at St John's Jerusalem.

Looking across the Cottage Garden towards the Tower of Sissinghurst Castle, which contains the room in which Vita wrote, you can imagine few more quintessentially English and romantic scenes. But Sissinghurst is a fine example of things rarely being as they first appear. Sissinghurst is a dream today, a vision of beauty and a celebration of nature, but it is no fairy-tale castle. It only became known as 'le chateau' because that is how the French prisoners of war interred here during the Seven Years' War between 1756 and 1763 knew it. Before that, in Saxon times, it was a pig farm.

Such was the transformation achieved by Harold and Vita that the garden today is a multi-faceted gem, each garden room a thing of beauty, romantic and intimate, offering up delightful glimpses into the next. Far from being a consolation prize, Sissinghurst is a crowning glory.

Opposite: The Purple Border in June with lupins, roses, clematis and hardy geraniums.
Above left: Entrance to the White Garden. The gardens are designed as a series of rooms with 'doors' in walls and hedges through which another interesting vista can be discovered.
Left: The Cottage Garden at Sissinghurst is an intimate, enclosed area overlooked by South Cottage, a private space where the couple had their bedrooms and Harold his book room.

THE EAST

military research scientists tested the capabilities of aircraft, weaponry and atomic bomb technology here. They evaluated aircraft, guns and bomb-sights, practised night navigation and developed a huge range of projects to address technical difficulties experienced in action. Bomb ballistics was a key area.

The Atomic Weapons Research Establishment occupied the spit between 1953 and 1971. It constructed the bridges, laboratories and many test structures, including the distinctive 'pagodas', many of which remain in place today and are scheduled monuments. The pagodas were designed to absorb accidental explosion and vent gases in a controlled manner. As the trials involved high explosives, the hard roof of the 'pagodas' was designed to contain the flying debris. However, there was no accidental explosions so we will never know if it would have worked.

The Establishment proposed tests to simulate what would happen to the bombs when they were transported and stored as well as used, but defence departments suffered economic cutbacks and many such projects were cancelled or developed in partnership with the US rather than alone. The last tests at Orford Ness were run in 1971.

After the defence teams left, Orford Ness eventually became a medium-wave radio station best known for transmitting the BBC World Service to continental Europe. It only ceased operations in 2010.

Today, access to the site is restricted – both to protect the precious habitats here and to protect an unwary public from stepping on any discarded military debris. However, visitors with tickets can visit a number of the historic buildings, including the former site headquarters, where there is a real (decommissioned) nuclear bomb on display. There's also the Black Beacon. Supposedly it was a marine radio beacon; in reality it housed an experimental airfield location device for military aircraft.

Opposite: View of the pagodas, relics from atomic research during the Cold War, from the saltings west of Stony Ditch, Orford Ness.
Top: The Bailey Bridge at Orford Ness is a reminder of the military presence here. This is in fact a new one, put in by the Trust in 1995 on the site of an earlier bridge.
Above: This marine radio beacon from 1929 was actually part of a secret plan to develop an airfield location system for military aircraft.

Sutton Hoo, Suffolk

Shortly before the outbreak of the Second World War, archaeologist Basil Brown unearthed the ship burial of an Anglo-Saxon king and his extraordinary treasures. They had lain undiscovered for 1,300 years. It's the largest haul ever found in Northern Europe, and it transformed previous ideas about life in this era.

The area around Sutton Hoo is a graveyard of rich and eminent Anglo-Saxons. It has been inhabited since Neolithic times. By the time of the Anglo-Saxons, southern Britain was divided into small independent kingdoms of a pagan people who worshipped multiple gods and buried or cremated their dead with their possessions. The grave field at Sutton Hoo contained about 20 barrows – it's impossible to be sure, since many are eroded. Those in the royal graveyard are thought to have belonged to extremely wealthy or prestigious people, since all were buried with precious items – weapons, gaming pieces, the remains of animal sacrifices, drinking vessels. One is the grave of a man buried with his sacrificed horse, another a child buried with a belt buckle and tiny spear.

All this is impressive enough, but the main reason for Sutton Hoo's renown is the ship burial. It was missed by looters who raided the site in earlier times, and only came to light when Edith Pretty, a wealthy widow living nearby with an inheritance and an interest in archaeology, organised an excavation in 1938. She commissioned Basil Brown, a self-taught archaeologist from Suffolk who worked for the local museum. In 1939 Brown discovered an iron rivet he recognised as belonging to a ship. He and his colleagues – who

Right: Sunset over one of the burial mounds at Sutton Hoo.

Left: The Nave looking to the Chancel of Whipsnade Tree Cathedral. In 1930 Edmund wrote: 'As we drove south through the Cotswold Hills on our way home ... I saw the evening sun light up a coppice of trees on the side of a hill. It occurred to me then that here was something more beautiful still and the idea formed of building a cathedral with trees.'

Mount Stewart, County Down

The Neo-classical home of the Londonderry family for more than 250 years, Mount Stewart has just emerged from a three-year restoration project that shows off its magnificent collections to great effect. A selection of the priceless family silver is on display at the east end of the Central Hall, dating from 1694 to the mid-twentieth century. No fewer than 11 portraits by Georgian fine artist Sir Thomas Lawrence hang in the restored Drawing Room. Also look out for the famous Stubbs painting, which shows the racehorse Hambletonian after he won the Match Race at Newmarket racecourse on 25 March 1799.

Waddesdon Manor, Buckinghamshire

Waddesdon is stuffed to bursting with beautiful and precious objects. It was created by Baron Ferdinand de Rothschild, who was passionate about French eighteenth-century collections – especially furniture, porcelain and textiles. The family built houses, created interiors and collected to such an extent that the term *Le Goût Rothschild* now describes the detailed, lavish style of interior decorating for which they became known. Look out for Savonnerie carpets, tapestries from the Beauvais workshops, magnificent English paintings and French porcelain and furniture.

Knole, Kent

Knole's internationally important collection includes paintings by Gainsborough and Reynolds, two state beds and a set of silver furniture. Charles, 6th Earl of Dorset, acquired royal chairs, footstools, sofas and beds (that had variously belonged to a number of monarchs since James I), which he put on display at Knole. 'They are lovely, silent rows for ever holding out their arms and for ever disappointed' wrote Vita Sackville-West in *Knole and the Sackvilles*, her history of the family home she was unable to inherit because of her gender.

GAZETTEER

THE MIDLANDS

Attingham Park
Atcham, Shrewsbury, Shropshire, SY4 4TP
01743708123
attingham@nationaltrust.org.uk

Berrington Hall
near Leominster, Herefordshire, HR6 0DW
01568615721
berrington@nationaltrust.org.uk

Biddulph Grange Garden
Grange Road, Biddulph, Staffordshire, ST8 7SD
01782517999
biddulphgrange@nationaltrust.org.uk

Birmingham Back to Backs
55–63 Hurst Street/50–54 Inge Street, Birmingham,
West Midlands, B5 4TE
01216667671
backtobacks@nationaltrust.org.uk

Calke Abbey
Ticknall, Derby, Derbyshire, DE73 7LE
01332863822
calkeabbey@nationaltrust.org.uk

Clumber Park
Worksop, Nottinghamshire, S80 3AZ
01909544917
clumberpark@nationaltrust.org.uk

Croome
near High Green, Worcester, Worcestershire,
WR8 9DW
01905371006
croome@nationaltrust.org.uk

Formby
Victoria Road, near Formby, Liverpool, L37 1LJ
01704878591
formby@nationaltrust.org.uk

Kinver Edge and the Rock Houses
Holy Austin Rock Houses, Compton Road, Kinver,
near Stourbridge, Staffordshire, DY7 6DL
01384872553
kinveredge@nationaltrust.org.uk

Packwood House
Packwood Lane, Lapworth, Warwickshire, B94 6AT
01564782024
packwood@nationaltrust.org.uk

Stoneywell
Whitcrofts Lane, Ulverscroft, Leicestershire, LE67 9QE
01530248040
stoneywell@nationaltrust.org.uk

Wightwick Manor and Gardens
Wightwick Bank, Wolverhampton, West Midlands,
WV6 8EE
01902761400
wightwickmanor@nationaltrust.org.uk

Woolsthorpe Manor
Water Lane, Woolsthorpe by Colsterworth, near
Grantham, Lincolnshire, NG33 5PD
01476862823
woolsthorpemanor@nationaltrust.org.uk

The Workhouse, Southwell
Upton Road, Southwell, Nottinghamshire, NG25 0PT
01636817260
theworkhouse@nationaltrust.org.uk

THE NORTH

Aira Force and Ullswater
near Watermillock, Penrith, Cumbria, CA11 0JS
01768482067
ullswater@nationaltrust.org.uk

Allan Bank and Grasmere
Allan Bank, Grasmere, Ambleside, Cumbria,
LA22 9QB
01539435143
allanbank@nationaltrust.org.uk

Ambleside
near Windermere, Cumbria
01539446027
windermere@nationaltrust.org.uk

Borrowdale and Derwent Water
near Keswick, Cumbria
01768774649
borrowdale@nationaltrust.org.uk

Buttermere Valley
Buttermere, near Cockermouth, Cumbria, CA13 9UZ
01768774649
buttermere@nationaltrust.org.uk

Cragside
Rothbury, Morpeth, Northumberland, NE65 7PX
01669620333
cragside@nationaltrust.org.uk

Derwent Island and House (see also Borrowdale and Derwent Water)
Keswick Lakeside car-park, Lake Road, CA12 5DJ (pay
and display car-park – not National Trust)
01768774649

Dunham Massey
Altrincham, Cheshire, WA14 4SJ
01619411025
dunhammassey@nationaltrust.org.uk

Dunstanburgh Castle
Craster, Alnwick, Northumberland, NE66 3TT
01665576231
dunstanburghcastle@nationaltrust.org.uk

Embleton and Newton Links
Low Newton by the Sea, Alnwick, Northumberland,
NE66 3ED
northumberlandcoast@nationaltrust.org.uk

Farne Islands
Near Seahouses, Northumberland
01289389244
farneislands@nationaltrust.org.uk

Fountains Abbey and Studley Royal Water Garden
Fountains, Ripon, North Yorkshire, HG4 3DY
01765608888
fountainsabbey@nationaltrust.org.uk

Hadrian's Wall and Housesteads Fort
Near Bardon Mill, Hexham, Northumberland,
NE47 6NN
01434344525
housesteads@nationaltrust.org.uk

Picture Credits